GOING PLACES

GOING PLACES

The Young Traveler's Guide and Activity Book

HARRIET WEBSTER

Illustrated by Gail Owens

Macmillan/McGraw-Hill School Publishing Company

New York ▪ Chicago ▪ Columbus

This edition is reprinted by arrangement with Aladdin Books, an imprint of Macmillan Publishing Company.

Cover design by Vikki Sheatsley

Macmillan/McGraw-Hill School Division
10 Union Square East
New York, New York 10003

Printed in the United States of America

ISBN 0-02-179521-5 / 5, L.11A

2 3 4 5 6 7 8 9 WES 99 98 97 96 95 94 93

for eight great Gloucester kids:
Erika, Elizabeth, Clea, Abby, Susannah,
Nathan, Jamie, and Ray

Contents

Introduction

Going Places is a book for kids who like to experience the sounds, smells, sights, and tastes offered by different places. It is not a guidebook to anywhere in particular. It's a guide to making the most of your trip opportunities, whether you're traveling ten miles or two thousand miles from home.

In the chapters that follow, you will learn how to get the information you need to help your family plan a trip. You will find out the answers to questions that commonly come up when you travel, such as "Where do zoos get their animals?" and "What's under a manhole cover?" Beyond that, you will find ideas to think about and things to do in an airport, on a camping trip, in an art museum, even waiting in line.

The world is a big and wondrous place. We hope that *Going Places* will encourage you to look at familiar spots with a fresh eye and to approach new ones with excitement and enthusiasm.

ONE

Planning Your Trip

Getting ready for a trip can be almost as much fun as taking one. The first step is to gather information, so you'll know as much as possible about the area you're going to visit. Once your research is completed, it's time to make an itinerary, a detailed plan describing where you'll go and how you'll get there, where you'll stay, and what you hope to see and do.

In preparing for your trip, you might also want to think about how you'll remember it when it's over. One easy way to preserve your memories is to write yourself a picture postcard each day of the trip, and mail it to yourself. When you get home you'll have an illustrated journal of your experiences waiting for you right there in your mailbox.

Gathering Information

The more you know about your destination, the more you'll be able to enjoy your trip. That's because planning ahead allows you to discover the possibilities that are awaiting you. You can plan your time to make sure you don't miss the places and activities at the top of your list. It isn't much fun to travel to a distant city and discover that the museum you wanted to visit is closed on Mondays or that the baseball game you hoped to see is sold out. Planning ahead can help you avoid disappointments like these. It can also open your eyes to activities and attractions you may not even have heard of when your family decided where to go.

To begin your research, head for your local library. Your librarian can help you find the names and addresses of local, state, and regional tourist bureaus and chambers of commerce that serve the areas you plan to visit. Write to them well in advance of your trip, requesting brochures, maps, calendars of events, and any other information you need (how to get tickets to that ball game, for example). It is their business to promote tourism, so they will be happy to help you.

Once you have collected and studied the material, you can sit down with your parents and plan what you would like to do each

day of the trip. If you are traveling by car, you may want to plan brief side trips to places of interest along the way.

Your librarian can also help you find books to read that will help you learn about the history of the place you are going to visit and about people who lived there. The librarian may also know about works of fiction that are set in the area you plan to visit.

Packing Your Backpack

Whether your travels will last a day or a month, you will want to take along a small backpack containing supplies that will make the trip more enjoyable. The items you pack will depend upon your interests and where you are going. If you are traveling a long distance, a small radio or tape recorder equipped with a headset can help you pass the time. A deck of cards is also useful, and so is a good book, especially if the story relates to your destination.

To keep a record of your trip, take along a notebook and several pens or pencils. Write the date at the top of the page, and perhaps a note describing the weather. Then use the notebook as a journal, recording any thoughts or impressions you wish to store away. Some people like to write in their journals at the same time

each day, perhaps before going to sleep at night. Others prefer to scribble notes throughout the day, whenever the mood strikes. Either way works well. If you want to write postcards to friends, enter their addresses in the back of your journal before you leave so they will be handy when you need them. If you like to draw, you may prefer to record your impressions in pictures; pack a sketchpad and some markers or other simple art supplies.

Traveling by car? Include a road map so that you will be able to keep track of your progress. If you are traveling by plane, add to your pack the free air-route map you will find in the seat pocket. Other handy items to include are small plastic bags (for collecting), white glue, and string, all of which come in useful at unexpected times. Consider bringing a small flashlight and a magnifying glass. If you plan to take photos, pack your camera and film in your backpack so that they're always nearby when you need them.

In supplying your backpack, the main idea is to stick to items that you want to have easily available throughout the day. But if you stuff it too full, you'll have trouble finding what you need. With a little practice, you will figure out what is right for you.

Six Ways to Keep Busy While Standing in Line

Standing in line is a sometimes annoying, often necessary part of taking trips. Important monuments, tourist attractions, and exciting rides just naturally draw crowds, as do popular restaurants and movies. Here are some ways to keep your mind busy while you wait for your turn.

1. Make up stories about the people around you.
2. Determine the mood of the people in the line. What do their expressions tell you about what they are feeling? Study their

body language. Is the kid ahead of you kicking up dirt with his heel because he's bored or angry at his parents for making him come along? What do people do with their hands when they're excited? When they're frustrated?

3. See if you can start a conversation with strangers in the line. Ask them if they've been here before, and where they're from. You might ask whether they have any tips to offer about other places in the area to visit, or if they can suggest a good place to get a hamburger.

4. Eavesdrop. Listen to what the people around you are saying. What do other people talk about while they wait in line? Why do people discuss the weather so much?

5. Take a survey. How many people in the line are wearing sunglasses? How many children under the age of six are in the line? How many people over the age of seventy? How does this compare to the line you stood in yesterday?

6. Bone up on the place you are about to visit by reading brochures and guidebooks. Then you'll know just what to look for.

Documenting Your Travels with Photographs

Lots of people love to snap pictures as they travel. They take photos of the famous places they visit, of family members and people they meet along the way, of pretty views. The pictures get developed, admired, and shoved into the back of a drawer. The problem comes when you pull them out a few years later, and you may have forgotten where they were taken or who the strangers are. If you like to take lots of pictures (and taking lots is one of the best ways of getting some really good ones), promise yourself that you'll take the time to sit down and label your pictures and mount them in an album as a permanent record of your experience.

For a complete record of your trip, you might consider expanding your photo album into a scrapbook by combining your pictures with other bits of memorabilia you have collected on the trip: ticket stubs, clippings from a local newspaper, menus, brochures, pressed flowers, postcards, theater programs, and the like. To make it even more complete, use index cards to write out your memories about the places and people you visited and the things you did. Then add these to your album.

Another way to use photographs to document your trip is to specialize. If you visit a large city, for example, you might decide to concentrate on photographs of skyscrapers. If you visit a national park, you might choose to take pictures of all the types of trees you see. You might decide to photograph only people: the man who pumps gas, the farmer on the tractor, the elderly man feeding pigeons in the park, the policeman controlling the traffic. Whatever

your subject, try to get shots from a distance as well as close-ups. Snap your subject at different times of day, from different angles.

Still another way to approach photography is to take pictures with the purpose of using them to tell a story. You might photograph the view from your hotel window at intervals throughout the day, showing how the mountains look at dawn, at midmorning, at noon, in the late afternoon, at sunset, and at dusk. Or take pictures of the woods before, during, and after a snowstorm. If you are spending a week at the seashore, shoot the same strip of shoreline at the same hour each day, reflecting the way in which shifting tides affect the contours of the beach. If you are going on a fishing expedition, take photos of your family carrying the necessary gear, baiting hooks, casting the line, pulling in the fish, gutting it, cooking it, and eating it.

After you have had your pictures developed, label, arrange, and mount them. What do they tell you about the place you have visited? Do your photos bring back memories of sounds, smells, or tastes? Postcards usually provide an excellent record of major sites and scenes. What is special about *your* photographs is that they represent what caught *your* eye. They are a record of your unique point of view and they represent your personal experience.

What Does "Old" Really Mean?

Here's a quick experiment to try. Write the word "old" across the top of a piece of paper. Now jot down any thoughts, things, places, ideas, or people the word brings to mind.

Now think about the words you've written. Sometimes "old" means useless, broken, or out of style. At other times, it implies wisdom, great value (as in a very old baseball card), or fragility. Do the words on your list fall into these categories?

"Old" can also mean steeped in history, and that's the way it is used when applied to many places that attract tourists. You visit the natural history museum to see the exhibit of dinosaur fossils. They're certainly old. Perhaps you will visit homes where famous people were born and lived. You might visit a battlefield, a one-room schoolhouse, a fort, a clipper ship, a recreated village. All of them are called "old," but what does that really mean? After all, Abraham Lincoln's stovepipe hat is certainly old, but it's nowhere near as old as George Washington's false teeth. Old is a comparative term. It implies that something is older than something else. An old house in Florida might be a couple of hundred years younger than an old house in New England, but that's because Florida was settled much later than New England.

One way to keep a clear picture of how long ago one event occurred compared to another is to draw a time line depicting the events, places, and artifacts you encounter on your trip. Use a roll of paper about six feet long, or staple together lengthwise six (or more) pieces of blank paper. Figure out the earliest period in time represented on your trip (for example, the date the Pilgrims landed at Plymouth Rock) and the most recent (*Old Ironsides* launched). Make a broad horizontal line across the center of your long strip of

paper. Write 1620 at the far left edge and then write 1797 at the far right edge, noting the significance of each date. Write 1625, 1650, 1675, 1700, 1725, 1750, and 1775 (or any guide numbers you choose) along the line at even intervals. Now you have a time line representing the period of history covered on your trip.

Each time you visit a place, be it the *Mayflower II,* the recreated Plymouth Plantation, *Old Ironsides,* Paul Revere's house, the Old North Church, the Bunker Hill Monument, or the Boston Tea Party Museum, enter a brief description of the site and its significance at the appropriate place on your time line. You might also decide to glue on postcards or other mementoes, or to illustrate the time line with your own drawings. Roll it up and fasten it with paper clips whenever you finish working on it. When you get home, you will have a historical record of your travels ready to mount on your wall as a mural. Best of all, you'll have a visual reminder that keys you in on how different moments in history relate to each other. Sometimes old is just not new, and sometimes it is ancient!

TWO

The Lay of the Land

Geography is the science that focuses on the topography or surface features of the earth, such as rivers, mountains, and deserts. Geographers also study the flora and fauna of different surroundings, natural resources, climate, population patterns, and political divisions. The best way to become an amateur geographer is to study, use, and make different types of maps.

Getting a Grip on the U.S.A.

Our country stretches 1,600 miles from north to south and 2,800 miles from east to west. Coast to coast, that's nearly the same distance as from New York to London, passing over the Atlantic Ocean. Or think of it this way: If you traveled by car at a steady speed of sixty miles an hour, never once stopping for a break, it would take nearly forty-seven hours to cross the country. If you were to choose jet travel instead, the nonstop trip would take about five hours. From the edge of the Atlantic Ocean, you'd head inland and soar above the gentle rises of the Appalachian Mountains and the fertile farmlands of the Midwest. Depending upon your route, you might catch a glimpse of the Great Lakes to the north. Farther west, you'd look down on the endless prairies and cattle-grazing land. On the southern route, you might see desert below. Then you'd climb above the snow-capped Rockies before passing over the lush green valleys of California and the shores of the great Pacific Ocean.

That's a lot of territory! Think how challenging a cross-country expedition must have been for our forebears, who made their treks without the benefit of modern transportation. Parts of the Great Plains were so featureless and so flat that settlers drove stakes into the ground to show others where to go. Even today, that area is called Staked Plains. Another way they left directions for those who would follow was to sprinkle mustard seeds through the western valleys in the hope that a trail of bright yellow plants would signal the way.

There were other difficulties, too. The main road through the Sierra Nevada Mountains in California, for example, winds through a mountain pass that used to be so narrow that the settlers had to take their wagons apart and carry them through piece by piece. Then they'd have to reassemble them on the other side before continuing on their journey.

In addition to its size and varied terrain, the U.S.A. also has big variations in climate, ranging from warm, temperate zones to frozen lands. There are great differences, too, in moisture. One of the most significant boundaries is the 20-inch rainfall line, a divider running north to south almost right through the middle of the country. Areas to the east of the line tend to receive 20 inches or more of annual rainfall, while those to the west receive less than 20 inches. This means that farming tends to be easier to the east, which results in a larger population. To the west of the line, lack of rainfall means that farmers have to rely on expensive man-made watering systems to meet the needs of their crops. That's why they often turn to raising cattle, which requires much less water.

The northwest coast, however, is a spectacular exception to the 20-inch rainfall line. Here, the heavy Pacific rains support the growth of huge sequoias and fir trees. Some, commonly called redwoods, are over 3,000 years old, which makes them some of the oldest living things on earth. It means that some were seedlings back when Troy fell. By the time Rome was built, they were already forest giants. Some are so broad that arches have been cut through the trunks to allow cars to pass through.

Rivers are another important feature of our country. There are six great ones: the Mississippi, Missouri, Ohio, Columbia, Colorado, and Rio Grande. Taken together with the Missouri, its chief western branch, the Mississippi travels some 4,000 miles from its northern sources in the Rockies to its terminus in the Gulf of Mexico. That makes it one of the longest waterways in the world.

There is so much to explore in the U.S.A. that you need never run out of discoveries to make or places to explore. A good way to keep track of what you have seen and to build on your knowledge is to keep a naturalist's scrapbook (see page 40).

All about Maps

The earliest maps date back several thousand years. They were simply scratches in the dirt that primitive people used to show the way to water or food sources, or to home when home might have been only a cave. The oldest maps still in existence are etched sun-baked clay tablets from the ancient kingdom of Babylonia. The early Chinese painted maps of their empire on swaths of silk. The

PAPYRUS MAP OF EGYPTIAN GOLD MINE, 1320 B.C.

THE EARLIEST KNOWN MAP IS
A CLAY TABLET FOUND IN IRAQ.
IT WAS MADE ABOUT 2300 B.C.

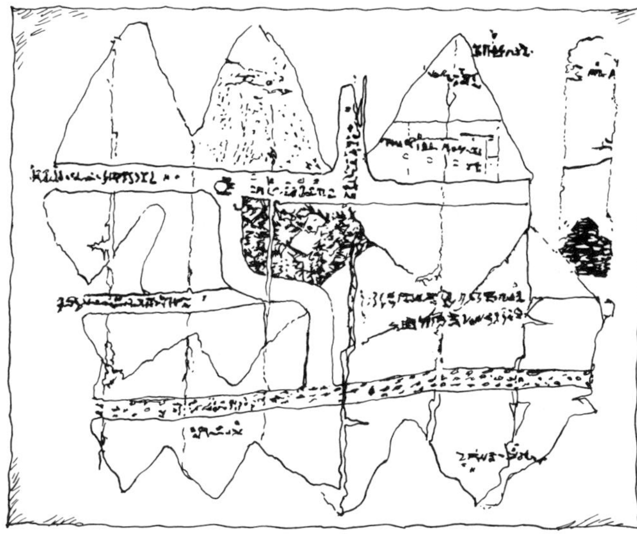

Polynesians wove maps or charts of the Pacific Ocean out of reeds and palm leaves. They tied on shells to show the location of islands and bent the reeds to show the direction of the waves and currents. People used whatever material was available to make their maps.

Maps offer an excellent way of keeping track of where you are going, where you have been, and what you have seen. To understand maps, you need to know some basic terminology, or "map language." Map language refers to all the names, numbers, symbols, lines, and colors that are used to illustrate details on a map. For example, each map includes a directional key showing the four directions: north, south, east, and west. North always points to the North Pole and south points to the South Pole. East indicates the direction where the sun rises and west indicates where it sets. If you want to make a map of your own town or neighborhood, you'll need to know which way is north. To figure that out, you'll need to use a compass, either bought or homemade.

Make Your Own Compass

To make your own compass, you will need a steel needle, a nonmetallic bowl about 12 inches in diameter (glass, china, or plastic will do fine), a cork or a chunk of Styrofoam, a magnet, and tape. Fill the bowl with water and put it in a place where it won't be near any large metal object. Pull your needle lengthwise across the surface of the magnet about a dozen times, always pulling in the same direction. To test your needle to make certain it's magnetized, see if it will stick to your refrigerator. It should pull or resist when you take it off. Now tape the needle to the cork or Styrofoam (to make it float). Put it in the bowl of water. The needle will line up in a north–south direction. To figure out which end is pointing north and which is pointing south, ask yourself where the sun rises in the morning. That will be to the east; the opposite (where the sun sets) will be to the west. Now, which end of the needle is pointing toward the North Pole and which is pointing toward the South Pole?

A compass works because magnets are pieces of iron that attract other materials that contain iron. One end of the magnet is attracted to the North Pole and the other to the South Pole. Try turning the bowl. What does the needle do?

Become a Cartographer

You can make your own atlas, or book of maps, to record your travels and observations. Then, you will be an amateur cartographer, the formal name for mapmaker. Your atlas can contain both ready-made maps and those you draw yourself from scratch. Here are some ideas to get you started.

Each map has a *key* or *legend* that explains the symbols used on the map. One of the most important parts of the key is the *scale*. Because maps are always much smaller than the area they represent, distance (how far apart two places are) has to be drawn to scale. This means that the mapmaker decides on a formula. He may decide that 1 inch on his map equals 100 actual miles. If he does that, the distance on his map between Boston, Massachusetts, and Miami, Florida, will be about 15 inches, because the real distance is about 1,500 miles. The distance between Boston and New York will be represented by about 2 inches, because it is about 200 miles. Scale allows the mapmaker to draw a picture that places locations in accurate proportion to each other.

To find out how far apart two places on a map are, measure the distance between them with a ruler or tape measure. Then multiply that number by the scale. If the scale is 1 inch = 10 miles, for example, and the distance between the two places that interest you is 4 inches, you can multiply 4 by 10 and you'll discover that the two places are approximately 40 miles apart. We say approximately because roads wind and twist and never make an absolutely straight path from one point to another. The distance you would travel is actually a little longer than 40 miles, but at least you'll be able to determine whether that destination would make a good day trip for your family or whether it should perhaps be saved for an overnight trip.

Often the key will include an elevation chart, which uses different colors to indicate the height of the land. One color will be used to show the land at sea level and other colors will be used to indicate deserts, plains, low mountains, and higher mountains. Sometimes a different shade is required to show land that lies below sea level, such as the floor of the Grand Canyon in Arizona. Another way to show what the land is like is to use different kinds of lines—jagged ones for high mountains, for example, and wavy ones for rolling, hilly areas. Some maps have depth charts as part of the key. Much like an elevation chart, a depth chart uses different colors to indicate the distance from sea level to the bottom of a lake, river, or ocean.

The key might also include a population chart, with a different type of shading used to indicate areas that are sparsely, moderately, and densely settled. Sometimes different typefaces are used to show the size of cities; usually the smaller the type, the smaller the population. Another symbol that frequently appears in the key is a star or other sign to indicate that a particular city is the state capital.

It's fun to invent a key. First, decide on the scale. Make certain the scale you choose is appropriate for the size of paper you plan to use and the area you wish to represent on your map. If you decide that 1 inch equals 2 miles, you won't be able to fit a map of your state on even a very large sheet, even if you live in Rhode Island. But if you are mapping your neighborhood, the same scale may not give you enough room for all the details you wish to include. It could, however, be just right for a map of a town you are visiting.

Then invent other symbols to stand for important places (restaurants where you've eaten, sites you've visited, trails you've hiked).

Here are some types of maps, both ready-made and home-made, that you might want to include in your atlas:

1. Road map (with your trip route marked)
2. A map of the United States (with the area you are visiting circled)
3. A map of the state you are visiting
4. A map of the town you are visiting
5. Trail maps or maps of attractions you have visited (including maps that show the layout of museums)
6. A map of your hotel or campground

The more detail you add to the maps, the better record they will provide of your travels. You might want to lend your atlas to a friend who is planning a similar trip.

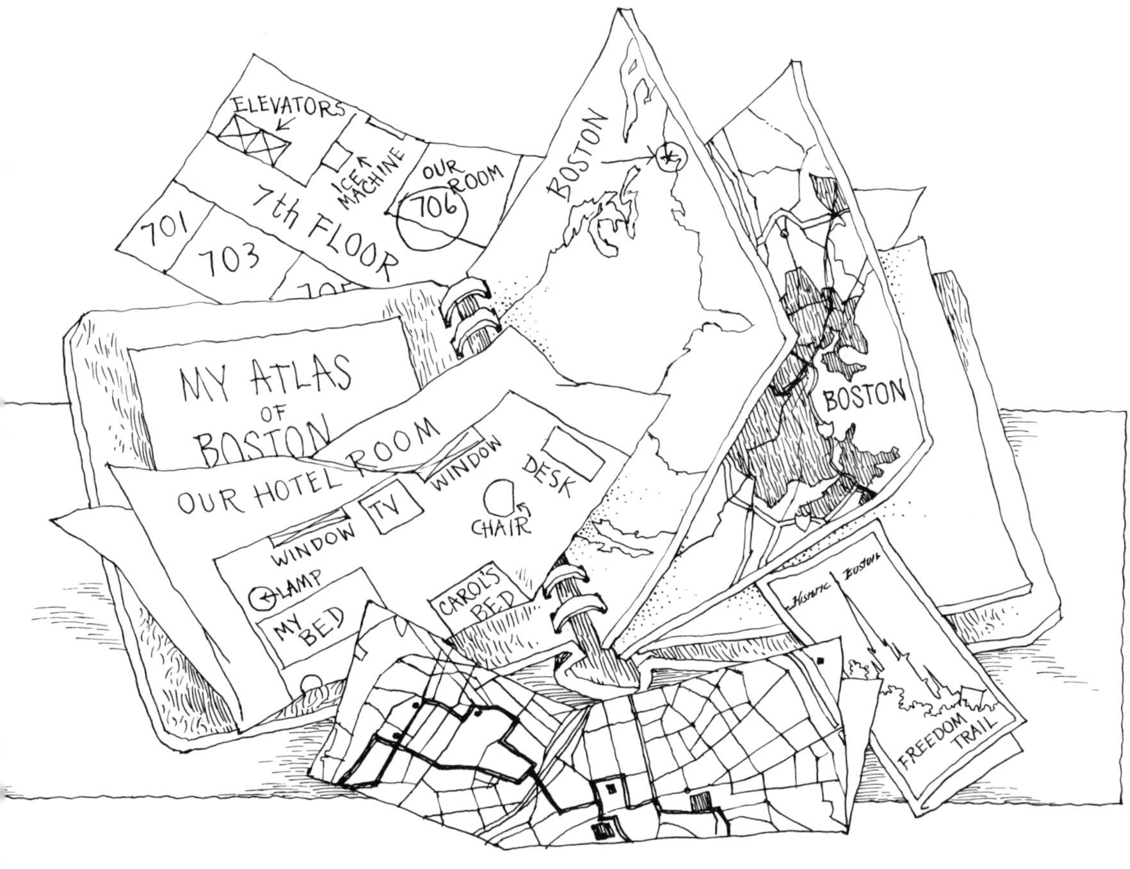

Make a Scale Ruler

If you plan to use one map frequently on your trip, a scale ruler can simplify your calculations. Place the edge of a strip of cardboard or a heavy piece of paper along the scale line on the key. Mark the points at the beginning and end of the scale line and mark the points in between, noting the number of miles represented by the distance between each of the marks. If the scale is 1 inch = 50 miles, your scale ruler will probably be marked out to show 50, 100, 150, and 200 miles. You can add numbers in between if you like (25, 75, 125, 175). By using the scale ruler, you can make a quick estimate of the distance between two points. Instead of asking how far it is, you'll be able to tell your family, "It's about fifty miles to Ocean City."

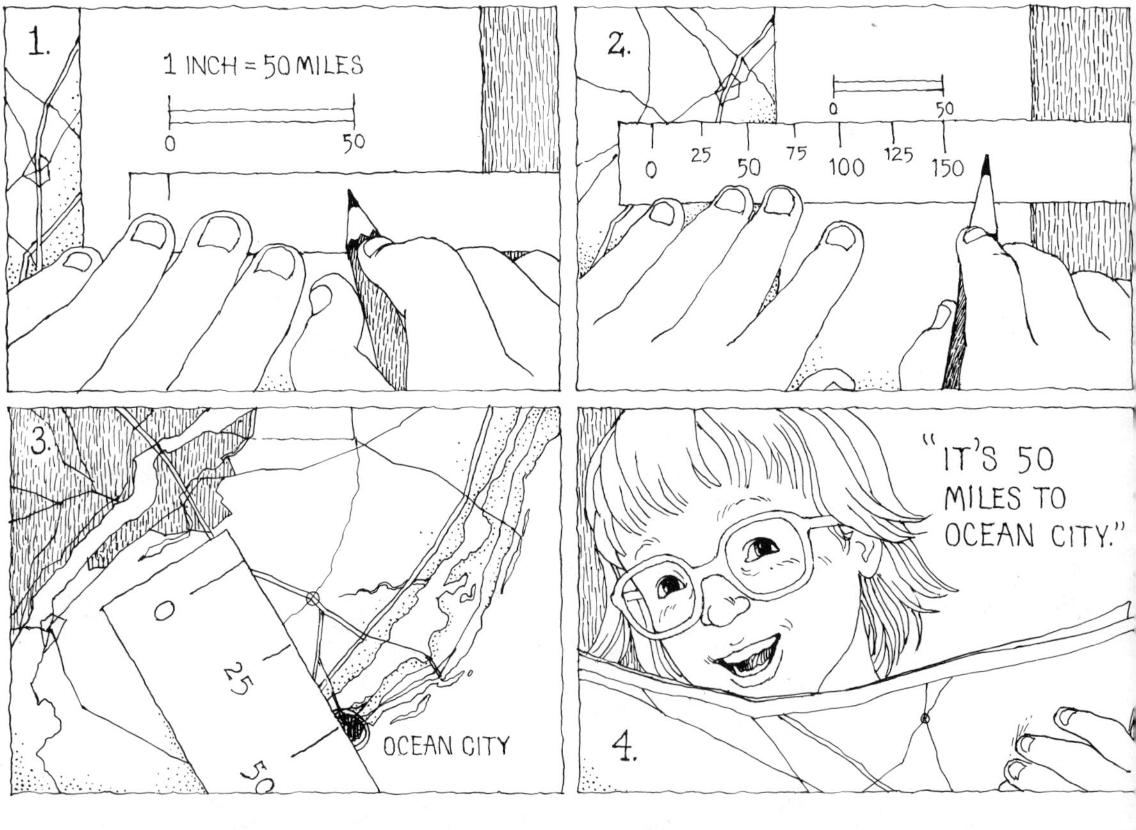

Some maps, like road maps, provide general information about an area, while others, like wildlife, history, or local maps, give specialized information. A local map provides a close-up look at a small area and usually includes natural features, landmarks, and man-made features, too. Small roads, a hospital, parks, an airport, schools, the public dock, and beaches will appear. General maps help you figure out where to go, how to get there, and what to look for on the way. Local maps show you what to do and where to explore once you arrive.

Where Do Places Get Their Names?

Place names are often rooted in the distant past. More than half of our states have Indian names, which the early European settlers borrowed from the Native Americans whom they met in the early years of our country's history. Arizona ("small spring") and Michigan ("great water") are two of these. Other names can be traced to the people who settled a particular part of our country. Colorado ("colored red") owes its name to the Spaniards who ventured there, while Louisiana was named for France's King Louis XIV. Maryland was named in honor of England's Queen Mary. Washington is the only state bearing a name that reflects American politics.

As you travel, make a list of unusual names, including parks, cities, streets, and bodies of water. As you visit museums and gather brochures and postcards, try to figure out where these names came from. Another good way to get information on names is to ask the people you meet: guides, the waitress in a restaurant, a policeman on the street. The stories behind the names will give you a better understanding of the area you are visiting.

THREE

On the Move

The way we get from one place to another affects what we see, do, and learn along the way. Sometimes we travel by boat or by train; more commonly, it is by car or airplane. These two methods of transportation have affected our travel plans in many ways. The development of the motel, for instance, is a direct result of the invention of the automobile. Travel by car has made it possible to go off the "beaten path," to see places not accessible to train or bus travelers. Jet travel allows us to vault time zones and to travel farther in shorter periods of time than our ancestors would ever have imagined.

Time Zones and Jet Lag

Travelers often cross from one time zone into another. Instead of waiting sixty minutes for 4:00 P.M. to become 5:00 P.M., you cross an invisible line and discover that time has immediately moved forward one hour. If you travel in the opposite direction, back into the former time zone, you will find that time has moved backward an hour. In order to make sense of this, let's take a look at the meaning of the term "time zone."

The globe is divided into twenty-four segments of equal size (think of them as the sections of an orange), each of which is called a time zone. The time in each zone is one hour earlier than it is in the adjoining zone to the east and one hour later than in the adjoining zone to the west. As the earth travels around the sun, it also rotates or turns on its axis. (Picture a stiff rod running straight through the center of the earth, from the North Pole to the South Pole.) When one segment receives direct sunlight (noon), the segment on the opposite side of the globe is in complete darkness (midnight). This is why the people on one side of the world are experiencing day while the people on the other side are experiencing night.

You can use a penlight, an orange, two toothpicks, and a pen to make your own model of the earth. With the pen, draw twenty-four lines from the top to the bottom of the orange, spacing them as evenly as possible. Then stick one toothpick in the top and the other in the bottom (one in the orange's "North Pole," the other in its "South Pole"), to indicate the earth's axis. Number the segments one through twenty-four. Have a friend hold the penlight pointing slightly downward on the surface of the orange. While the light remains stationary, you turn the orange slowly on its axis.

You'll notice that when segments one-two-three are in darkness, segments thirteen-fourteen-fifteen are receiving the most di-

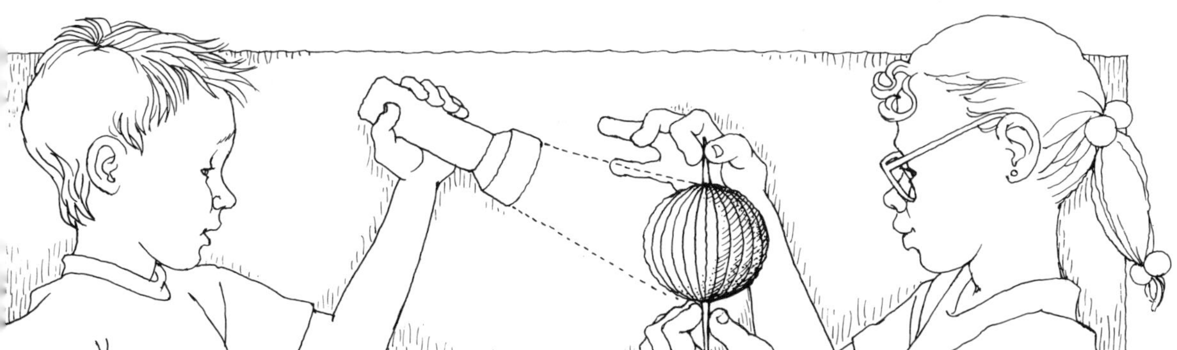

rect light. This is true for all the segments: the ones directly opposite each other are in the opposite light condition. This illustrates that at every moment the sun is rising and setting somewhere on the earth. As the light fades on one part of the orange's surface, it appears on another part. When kids in New York are getting ready for school, their peers across the world in Tokyo are getting ready for bed.

The world spins around on its axis once every twenty-four hours, rotating from east to west. But airplanes cannot fly as fast as the world turns. If you go from New York to San Francisco, departing at 8:00 A.M. and flying for five hours, you will arrive at 1:00 P.M. New York time, but it will be only 10:00 A.M. in California, because you have traveled three time zones to the west. By early evening, you might be running out of steam because even though the kids in San Francisco are just sitting down for dinner, your friends back in New York are climbing into bed.

By the time the clock says 9:00 P.M., you *feel* as if it's the middle of the night. This feeling is known as *jet lag.* Your body is still operating on New York time. In New York it's midnight and you would be fast asleep. The best way to get over jet lag, that sense of being out of tune with the time of day in your new location, is to get plenty of rest. Go easy on sightseeing and other activities the day you arrive so you can get caught up on your sleep and you'll soon feel as though you've always lived on this new time schedule.

On the other hand, you may have quite a different experience if you fly east from San Francisco to New York. Let's say you depart the West Coast at 2:00 P.M. and fly for five hours. When you arrive on the East Coast, the airport clock says 10:00 P.M. but it's only 7:00 P.M. back in San Francisco. Your parents tell you it's time for bed but your body says it isn't ready yet.

Look at the chart below. What do you think kids in Atlanta are doing while kids in San Diego are having dinner? If you flew from New York to Phoenix, departing at 3:00 P.M., and it took four hours, what time would it be when you arrived? What do you think children in Miami are doing when kids in Seattle are getting up? Have you figured those out? Then try two really tricky ones. What are kids in Milwaukee likely to be doing when kids in Topeka are getting ready for bed? If you leave Dallas on Thursday at 8:00 P.M. and fly for four hours, when will you arrive in Philadelphia? (Hint: It will be a different day.)

TIME ZONES
(based on standard time)

PACIFIC 7:00 A.M.	MOUNTAIN 8:00 A.M.	CENTRAL 9:00 A.M.	EASTERN 10:00 A.M.
Seattle	Helena	Milwaukee	New York
Portland	Denver	Chicago	Philadelphia
San Francisco	Santa Fe	Topeka	Atlanta
San Diego	Phoenix	Dallas	Miami

ANSWERS:

When it's 6:00 P.M. in San Diego, it's 9:00 P.M. in Atlanta, where the kids are probably getting into bed.

It is two hours earlier in Phoenix, so even though the trip took four hours, it would only be 5:00 P.M. when you arrive.

When it's 7:00 A.M. in Seattle, it's already 10:00 A.M. on the East Coast, so the Miami kids are probably in their classrooms, hard at work.

They're likely to be getting ready for bed, too. Both cities are in the same time zone.

You'll arrive at 1:00 A.M. the following morning.

Turnaround Time

While you are busy traveling to the airport and checking in for your flight, your aircraft is having an equally busy time. Perhaps it has just flown in from another part of the country or the world. Now it must be prepared for your trip. The period of time between the conclusion of one flight and the start of another is called "turn-around time." With a relatively small plane like the super-fast Concorde, turnaround time can be less than an hour, but with a jumbo jet that carries 350 passengers, it can be three hours. Let's look at what happens to the jumbo during that time.

When the plane comes to a halt on the runway at the end of a flight, the ground crew places blocks called chocks under its front wheels. Chocks look like small metal cages. When the plane lands, the brakes work very hard because they have to slow the weight of the entire plane. As a result, they become very hot. When the brakes are released, they cool down. Chocks prevent the plane from rolling when its brakes are released. (Have you ever seen blocks of wood jammed behind the tires of a parked truck to prevent it from moving if the brakes give? It's the same idea with the blocks used to brace plane wheels.)

Once the chocks have been positioned and the engines have been turned off, a ground power unit is attached to a socket near the front wheels of the plane. Because the auxiliary power unit (APU) on the plane is turned off while it is on the ground, the ground power unit is needed to run the plane's lights, heaters, and other systems while it is at rest.

Meanwhile, other members of the ground crew roll the mobile steps into place (unless you are at a jetport equipped with a tunnel entrance that opens directly into the door of the plane). The top of the steps is braced against the plane and the bottom is supported by a pair of metal "feet" that extend to hold the unit in place while passengers disembark.

While the passengers are getting off, baggage and freight are unloaded onto a freight elevator. Because there is so much cargo on a jumbo, most of the baggage travels in special containers that fit snugly into the hold of the plane. The baggage handlers then remove the containers rather than having to unload hundreds of individual suitcases.

Meanwhile, there is lots going on beneath the plane. The toilet-waste truck arrives to drain the holding tanks beneath the plane's chemical toilets. This is done by connecting large hoses from the truck to sockets underneath the aircraft that lead to the tanks. When empty, they are refilled with fresh chemicals. A water truck arrives to fill the water tanks, and an air-conditioning truck might drive up to pump fresh air of a comfortable temperature into the plane. (You'll discover that the air in the passenger cabin can become stale and humid after a long flight.)

Aircraft service trucks specially equipped with power-driven "scissors" arrive beside the plane to unload used supplies and to replace them with fresh ones: food, newspapers, towels, drinks, cleaning materials, and so on. The scissors, attached to the underside of the trucks, can raise the vehicles right up to the level of the plane door.

At the rear of the plane, a mobile platform that can be elevated to the top of the plane's tail is used to check out equipment and to make minor repairs. Maintenance engineers also check the plane's landing gear and tires.

About an hour and a half after landing, refueling begins. There are three fuel tanks located in each wing of the jumbo and the fuel must be evenly balanced among them. Measuring sticks that pull down from beneath the wings are used to determine how much fuel is left over from the preceding flight. Huge tanker trucks equipped with their own pumps carry the fuel out to the plane, where it is pumped in through hoses.

When you watch a jumbo refuel, you'll sometimes see only a small pumping rig, not a tanker truck. In this case, the fuel is stored underground and is fed into the plane through pipelines. Look carefully and you will see that the hose from the pumping rig is attached to a fuel outlet in the ground. Hoses at the other end of

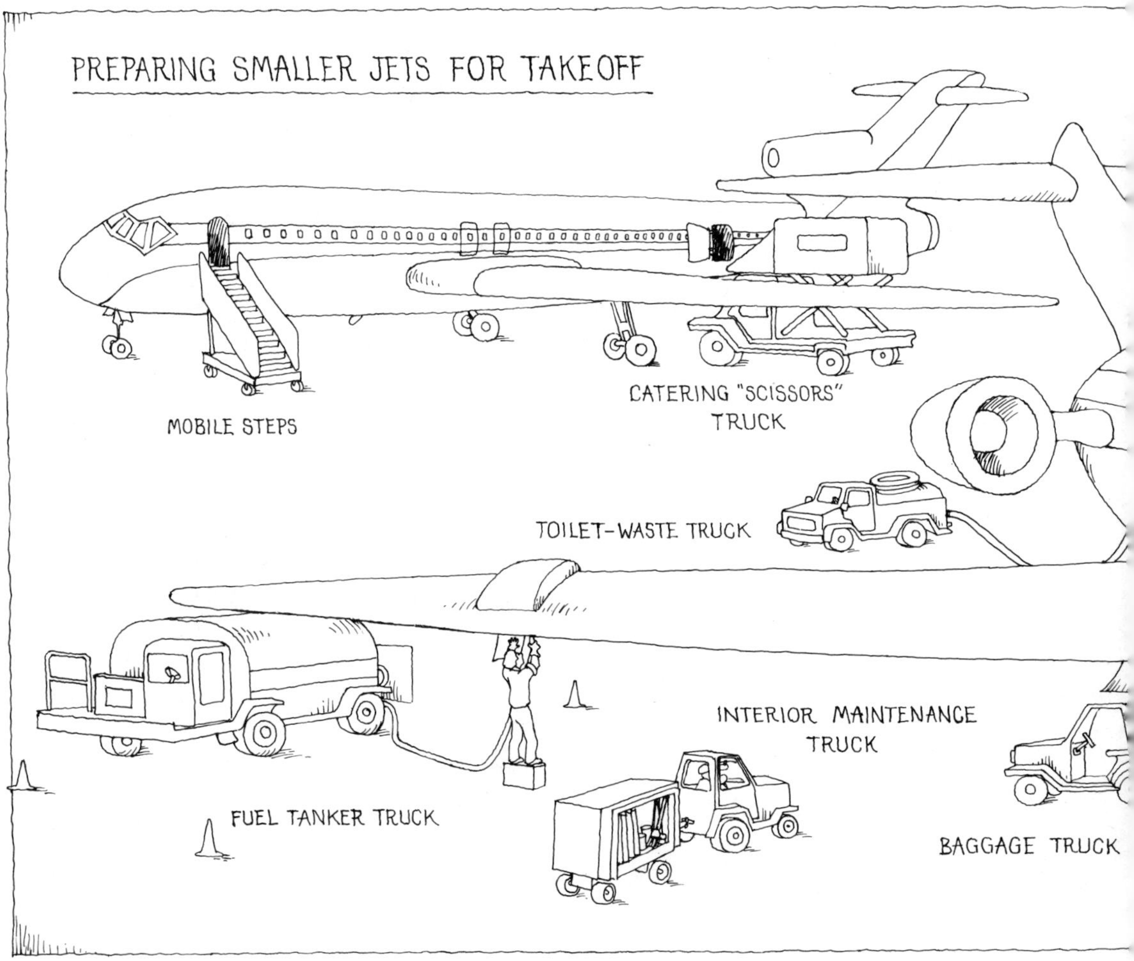

the rig lead up to the plane's fuel tanks. While the plane is being refueled, the flight crew checks the instruments aboard and the cabin staff makes certain that all emergency apparatus—oxygen masks, life vests, doors—is in its proper place.

Are you sometimes impatient while your car is being filled up at the gas station? Well, the jumbo can take up to 38,500 gallons of fuel. It takes about fifty minutes to pump a full load in. While you are waiting, see how many of the service vehicles and pieces of equipment mentioned here you can spot.

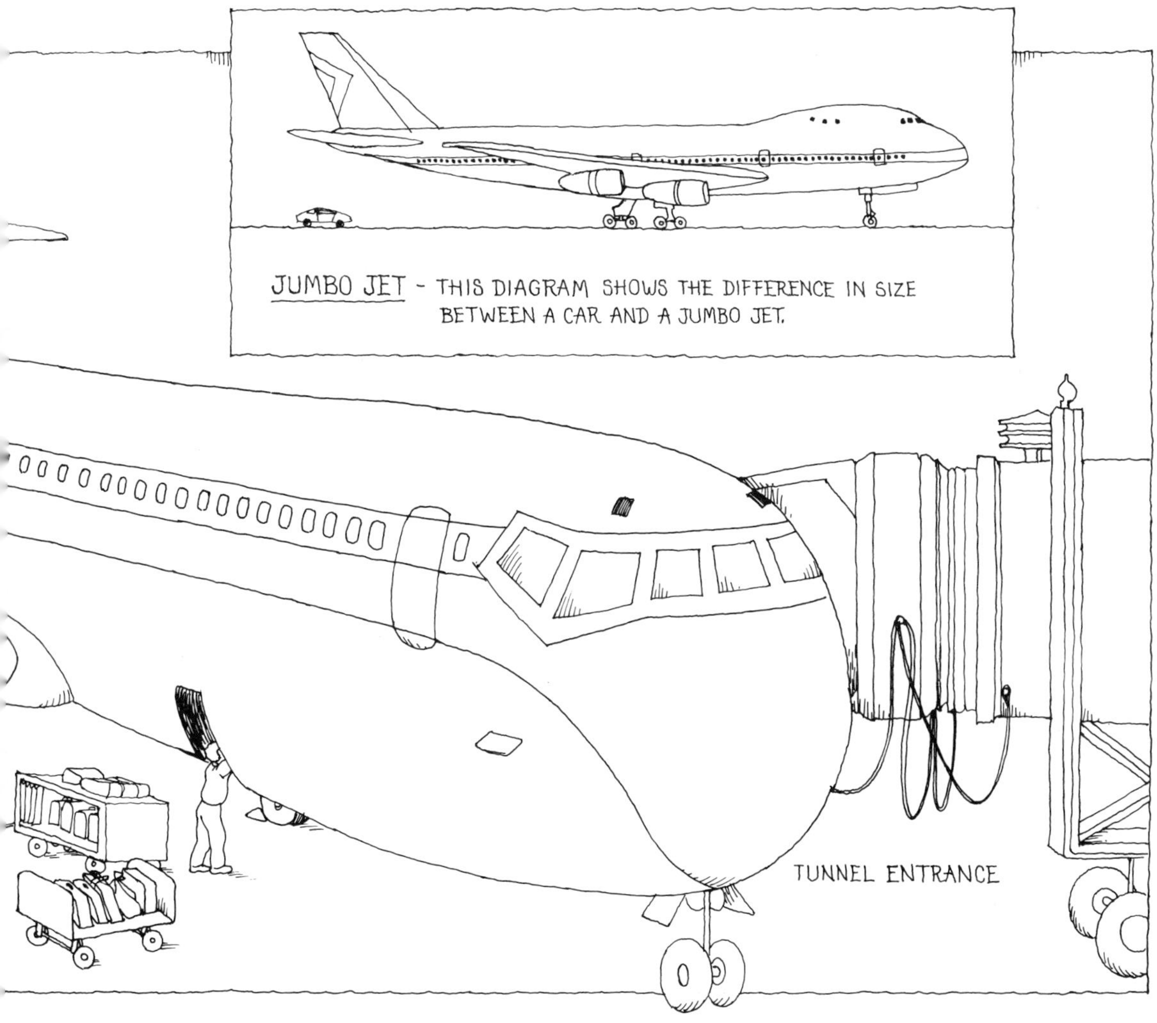

Baggage Handling

When you purchase airline tickets, you will probably be asked to arrive at the airport thirty minutes to a full hour before your flight is scheduled to depart. Air terminals are often very busy places where hundreds of passengers are trying to catch different flights at the same time of day. Ticket agents need time to check each passenger's ticket, to make seat assignments, and to issue boarding passes. They also need to take care of the baggage.

Your baggage does some traveling of its own even before your flight lifts off. When you check in, you place your suitcases and other large packages on a weighing station, being certain that each piece of luggage is clearly tagged with your name and address. The ticket agent will attach labels noting your flight number and destination. If your baggage exceeds the allowable amount, you will have to pay an extra charge. Once the bags are labeled and weighed, the agent will move them to a long conveyor belt that runs behind the check-in desks. In some airports, the agent will just push a button and the bags will move automatically from the weighing station to the main conveyor. In this case, the weighing station itself is actually a small section of conveyor belt.

Each section of conveyor belt is a long loop of canvas or rubber that is stretched between two rollers. As the rollers rotate, the belt or loop travels around them, moving whatever items have been placed on its surface. To get an idea of how this works, find a rubber band and two pencils. Stretch the rubber band between the

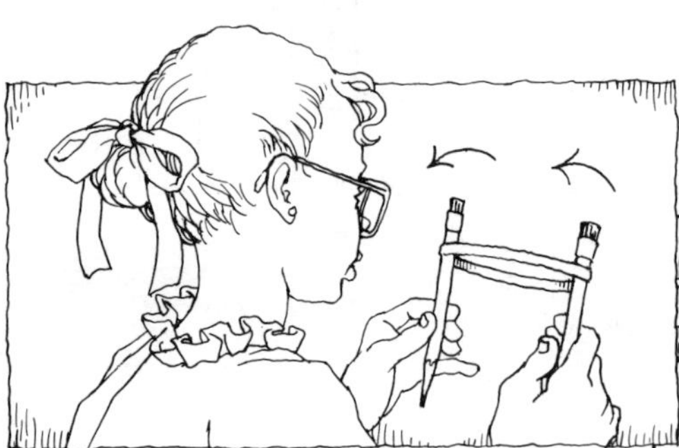

two pencils until it's just taut. Then roll the two pencils in the same direction and watch the rubber band travel around them. That's the way a conveyor belt moves.

The main conveyor belt carries the baggage down into the baggage-handling area, out of sight of passengers. Here it loads the bags onto the carousel, a circular conveyor. Photocells prevent the baggage from running into suitcases that are already circulating on the carousel.

Photocells are like electronic switches, operated by beams of light. Beams are flashed across strategic areas on both the main conveyor and the carousel. Let's imagine that two suitcases are traveling on a collision course. The red plaid one is going to knock over the tan one as it enters the carousel from the main conveyor. When the tan bag breaks the beam across the carousel just a couple of feet before the intersection with the main conveyor, and then the red plaid bag breaks the beam on the main conveyor also just before the intersection, the photocell signals a computer to stop the electrical current that powers that section of the main conveyor for two seconds, until after the tan bag passes the intersection. Collision averted, the red plaid bag then enters the carousel.

Baggage handlers unload baggage from the carousel and place it on trailers, to be driven onto the airfield for loading into the hold of the appropriate plane. Suitcases destined for travel on jumbo jets are first loaded into large containers, which are then loaded into the planes.

When a plane arrives at its destination, it is unloaded and the baggage is placed on another conveyor belt, which carries it to a carousel in the passenger baggage claim area. Here passengers locate their own bags, searching for them among the hundreds that sometimes circulate on the carousel, all having traveled on the same flight.

The large number of pieces of baggage that travel on a single flight is one reason why it is important to mark your bags clearly. You may think you are the only one traveling with a green suitcase that has a blue stripe or with a cherry-red backpack, but once you see the contents of a jumbo jet you will probably realize that your baggage is not so unusual. If you want to really make your suitcase stand out for easy locating, you might want to put a large, bright, and unusual decal on the outside.

Where Did Motels Come From?

Before there were cars, Americans traveled largely by train. They went where the tracks took them and they stayed in the hotels that the railroad companies built in the towns they served. With the development of automobiles in the early 1900s, families suddenly discovered that they could get off the beaten tracks. No longer were their vacation plans determined by the railroad routes. From 1910 to 1920, hundreds of thousands of families explored the countryside, sleeping in tents or in their cars.

Autocamping, or "gypsying" as it was sometimes called, soon led to health and environmental problems. People got sick from drinking impure water, and they often left litter and garbage behind. Arguments arose with property owners, who got tired of having just anyone park or pitch a tent on private land whenever and wherever he or she felt like it. Local merchants, on the other hand, wanted to increase their business by encouraging tourism, so that the visitors would spend money in their stores and restaurants. It was clearly time for some rules.

Town officials needed to find a way to protect the rights of the property owners and to satisfy the economic interests of the merchants at the same time. They found a solution by creating free municipal campgrounds. Towns would set aside areas where travelers could take advantage of a free place to camp. Located on the outskirts of towns, the campgrounds were usually supplied with electricity, hot showers, and central kitchens.

This worked at first, but soon towns were straining their budgets to provide more attractive campgrounds than neighboring towns'. Hoboes and impoverished wanderers began to make the campgrounds their homes, which tended to drive away the middle-class tourists who had money to spend in the local stores. As a result, the public campgrounds began to charge fees. That opened the door to private entrepreneurs, who could now compete with the public facilities. It also marked the beginning of the motel industry.

Eager to attract tourists, the entrepreneurs built cabins on their properties, creating early "motor courts." At first these were very basic, but soon owners started adding stoves, linens, and other extras. No longer was it necessary to take along a tent if a family wanted to take a trip into the country or to small towns. As the motor courts got fancier, they attracted even noncampers to out-of-the-way spots. These auto tourists preferred comfort to roughing it.

The motor courts could not have grown and thrived if it had not been for the increasing popularity of the automobile. In 1910, there were fewer than half a million car owners in the United States. By 1920, there were over eight million, and by 1925 the number jumped to more than seventeen million. In 1912, only twelve Americans drove across the country. In 1921, just nine years later, twenty thousand adventurous people made the trip. Do you know any elderly people who might remember what it was like to travel by car back in those days?

Three to six thousand auto camps existed during the 1920s. Some were tiny backyard operations, a handful of cabins or tent sites. Others were huge. Denver's Overland Park, established in 1915, could accommodate 2,000 auto campers and had a three-story clubhouse complete with grocery store, lunch counter, barber shop, laundry, showers, and more. A California entrepreneur named James Vail, whose San Luis Obispo motor court had so many extras that it seemed more like a hotel than a motor camp, is credited with being the first to use the word "motel," combining motor with hotel.

The next great growth spurt in the motel industry came in the 1950s, when the United States experienced a boom in highway construction. The new roads bypassed many of the old motor courts. With the increased number of motorists came the opportunity for increased profits, and soon large national companies began to construct motels near the highways, often attracting guests by appealing to their desire for the "old days." Motels in the Southwest were built to look like adobe missions, while a chain in the North built its units in the shape of log cabins. A resident of a particular area would pay the company a fee for the right to build and operate a branch of the motel. In exchange, the national office would provide the company logo or symbol, marketing advice, architectural plans, advertising, and other services. This system is called franchising. Tourists liked this arrangement because it gave them the personal attention of a local owner combined with the reassurance of knowing that the establishment had to meet certain standards set by the national company. Some of today's popular motel chains are owned by a single parent company; others continue to operate as franchises.

FOUR

Camping Out

Sleeping out in a tent is a special experience, whether you camp in your backyard, a popular campground, or an isolated spot deep in the woods. It provides an opportunity to get a feel for the outdoors, not just during the regular daylight hours, but at dawn and in the deep hours of the night as well. Camping out sharpens the senses. You will hear sounds, smell scents, and notice details that you have never been aware of before. If you love the woods, you will follow the advice of the great naturalist John Muir: "Leave behind nothing but footprints. Take nothing but memories." In other words, take care to gather up every bit of litter and please don't uproot the wildflowers. The better care we all take of the forests, the better they will serve us, now and in the years to come.

What Do I Do If I Get Lost?

It's lots of fun to explore a campground, but if you are staying at a large one, it's also easy to get confused and to have difficulty finding your campsite. You may think that yours is the one by the huge pine tree or the pile of boulders, but you might soon discover that there are tons of towering pines and heaps of big rocks that look very much alike.

When you set out to explore the campground, make sure you know the number of your site so that you can ask other campers for help if you get mixed up. It also makes sense to wear a whistle, which you can use to call for help if you wander off the path and get lost. Make sure that all members of your family know that three short blasts on the whistle is a universal signal for help. Use the signal only if you really need assistance. Another effective safety precaution is to always let an adult know where you are going when you leave your site, even if you are only walking to the showers or to the campground office to check the bulletin board.

Frequently campers get lost within a hundred yards of their campsite. Where the forest is dense, it can be impossible to see through the trees even for short distances. As soon as you begin to think that you might be lost, stop walking, stay in one place, and try to remain calm. Otherwise you may wander farther and farther from your campground in your efforts to find it. Be patient and you will probably be found quickly. And remember, use your whistle!

TAKE PRECAUTIONS WHEN LEAVING CAMP.

Observing Wildlife

Taking a walk in the country provides an opportunity to see animals in their natural setting. As a rule, animals flee from people. Their senses, particularly hearing and smell, are much keener than ours, so they often know that we are nearby before we see them. When taking a nature walk, then, try to be as inconspicuous as possible. Here are several ideas to help you make yourself less noticeable.

Camouflage is a type of disguise that helps you fade into your surroundings. Many animals possess natural camouflage. Polar bears blend into the snow and ice of their arctic background and snakes fade into the dust and pebbles of the desert landscape. By wearing clothes in colors that blend in with the setting you plan to explore, you increase the likelihood of spotting wildlife. Some animals, like the common field mouse, have very limited vision and can see clearly only a few inches ahead. Others, such as deer, have fine long-range vision. The better the vision of the animal, the more important your camouflage becomes.

If you want to camouflage yourself for an expedition in the woods, you will probably want to wear splotchy brown and green clothes that blend with the trees, bushes, and brambles. Store-bought camouflage wear is fine, but you can also make your own. Here's how to do it.

Camouflage Shirt and Pants

You will need: Rubber gloves, Rit dye (yellow and blue), plastic bucket or large bowl, an old white sports shirt, salt, spoon, and string. (You will not be able to use the bucket or bowl for anything else later, since it will be permanently stained, so choose an old one.)

1. Put on rubber gloves and prepare yellow dye in bucket or bowl, according to package directions, which call for salt.

2. Dye shirt, stirring with wooden spoon, following directions.

3. Rinse shirt in cold running water and then wash in hot soapy water until the water rinses clear.

4. To make a mottled pattern that will offer good camouflage in the woods, crumple each sleeve into a ball and wind string around it tightly in different directions. Then wad up pieces of the front and back of shirt and wind with string in the same way.

5. Prepare blue dye. Dye crumpled-up shirt. Unwind string before washing shirt in soapy water.

6. If you want darker colors, you can rewad the shirt and redye it before washing it out with soap.

NOTE: If you are using a green or brown shirt, begin with Step 4, using only the blue dye. For matching camouflage pants, follow the same procedure.

In addition to your dyed shirt and pants, it's a good idea to wear a dark-colored peaked hat. (You could dye an old baseball cap.) The peak will cast a shadow over your face, hiding it from animals' eyes. Another way to camouflage your face is to streak it with greasepaint (often sold in stores around Halloween) or even a

CAMOUFLAGE YOURSELF TO OBSERVE WILDLIFE.

lump of charcoal. Wear shoes that allow you to walk as quietly as possible, and be sure they don't have any shiny buckles to catch the light and scare the animals.

If you plan to watch wildlife at night, wrap a piece of red cellophane paper over your flashlight, securing it with a rubber band. Most mammals can barely detect red light.

Before heading out to make your observations, practice walking quietly and slowly. In addition to their keen sense of hearing, many animals are also sensitive to vibrations that travel through the ground. Decide where to place your feet before taking the next step, to avoid moving loose pebbles and crunching twigs underfoot. Use the cover offered by trees, bushes, and large rocks.

If you think you know where the animals are that you are trying to spot (let's say you've heard that moose come to drink from a particular pond at night), be sure to walk upwind of them. This means that you must be certain that if there is a breeze blowing, it comes toward you from the direction where you expect to find the animals. That way the animals don't pick up your scent and flee before you get a chance to see them.

Observing animals in the wild takes preparation, patience, and luck. But seeing a deer moving through the forest, instead of in a zoo, is well worth it!

Making Plaster Casts

Rabbits, skunks, raccoons, deer, and other animals all have distinctive footprints. To make a permanent record of the prints you find, cast them in plaster. The best tracks for this project are those you discover in dried-out mud. (If the mud is still wet and soft, the print will squoosh under the weight of the casting material and lose its shape.)

To make plaster casts, you'll need several short pieces of old wooden boards, plaster of Paris, water, a picture hanger or loop of wire for hanging, and a piece of terry cloth (such as an old towel).

After locating a clear set of tracks, use the boards to make a frame around them. Push the boards into the ground, leaving a wall or fence at least an inch high all around the prints. The length and shape of the walls determine the size of your casting.

Fill a bucket or bowl with water and add plaster of Paris, according to the instructions on the package. Mix them until they are smooth, using your hand or a heavy stick. Work quickly because the mixture will soon start to harden. When it is smoothly mixed, pour it into the wooden frame you've made. Then tap the walls of the frame with a stick to encourage air bubbles to float to the top. If you want to hang your casting, press in a picture hook or wire loop while the plaster is wet. Wait at least fifteen minutes, until the mixture hardens thoroughly. Then take the board frame apart and remove the casting from the ground. Turn it over and rub it gently with the terry cloth to remove bits of dirt.

Glue a label to the back to identify the prints: what animal made them and where you found them. A collection of plaster casts is a fine way to document the animal tracks you find on your camping trips, woodland walks, and visits to the country.

You can also make castings at the beach. Just be sure to bring

along enough fresh water to mix up the plaster of Paris. Salt water won't work!

Sand doesn't hold animal prints very well, but you can create a casting featuring the treasures you find along the shore. Dig a shallow hole in the hard wet sand. Press into it bits of shell, beach glass, driftwood, pebbles, and feathers. Your design will come out upside down. In other words, try to imagine what it would look like if you were staring up at it from beneath the ground. When you have the objects arranged the way you want them, pour plaster of Paris directly into the hole to a depth of about one inch. If you want to hang your casting on the wall, attach a picture hook or loop of wire to the back (the up side) while the plaster of Paris is still wet. Let it dry, and then pry the casting free, brushing off the loose sand on the front.

Naturalist's Scrapbook

Each time you visit a new body of water, a mountain, a forest, a desert, a cave, a canyon, or another natural feature, make a note of it in your book. Jot down the date, the name, the location (state, nearest town, distance from your home), and your observations. What did you do while you were there? Swim, fish, take a boat ride? Hike, camp, go bird-watching? What did the place look like? What was the weather like? List any plant or animal life observed. Include a drawing of the area or paste in postcards or photographs.

As your list of entries grows, try making comparisons between the places you have visited. Did you prefer Front Beach to Pebble Beach? Why? How did the sand on the beach differ? Did one beach have calm water and the other surf? What was the bottom like under the water? You can also make comparisons about a single place if you visit it more than once. How does it differ from one season to the next? From one year to another?

Some projects involve making a record of a single trip. When you return home, your work is completed. The naturalist's notebook is a different sort of project. It becomes richer and more valuable over time. As the seasons and the years pass, you will build a collection of impressions that will help you decide where you would like to go and what you would like to see in the future. It will be an excellent aid for you and your family as you plan future trips. You might also want to share it with friends who are making travel plans.

Stargazing

Stargazing is a great evening activity when you are on a camping trip or other visit to the country. Away from city lights, with the help of a star guide or chart and an active imagination, it's easy to pick out the constellations or star pictures high above. Have you ever lain on your back on a warm afternoon, staring up at the sky and finding pictures in the clouds? Well, you can create your own constellations in just the same way.

Some stars are brighter than others. In fact, stars are graded according to their brightness. The brightest (and there are only fifteen in our northern sky) are called first-magnitude stars; the faintest visible to the naked eye are those of the sixth magnitude. In creating your own constellation, it's easiest to anchor your picture to a first-magnitude star so you'll be able to find it again when you want to share it with someone or draw it on paper.

A good introduction to stargazing is a planetarium show at a science museum. A planetarium is a system of lights and lenses that projects an artificial night sky inside an auditorium with a ceiling shaped like a hemisphere or well-rounded dome. A dumbbell-shaped projector (containing individual projectors for the sun, the moon, the planets, and the stars) in the middle of the dome reproduces the motions of the heavenly bodies on the hollowed-out ceiling above. The earliest planetarium projector was developed by the German firm Carl Zeiss in the 1920s. A modern Zeiss system weighs two tons, has nearly 200 projectors, and contains about 29,000 parts. The planetarium enables us to see, within perhaps half an hour, motions in the sky that would actually take years to observe. Eclipses of the sun and moon are recreated and comets and meteorites dash across the sky.

FIVE

Visiting Museums

Museums come in all shapes and sizes. They serve as storehouses and showplaces for thousands of different kinds of treasures. Their collections are usually organized around a theme.

After you have visited a few museums, you may want to create your own. You can start by using a small table or bookcase as your exhibition area. Decide on your theme—perhaps your family history or a special interest, such as horses or baseball. Then gather together all the materials you can find related to your theme: photographs, magazine and newspaper clippings, artifacts (meaningful things, such as a lock of your grandmother's hair, a discarded horseshoe, or an autographed baseball). Label the items and arrange them until you like the way they look. You've just become a curator!

Museums

Museums help us appreciate and understand the world we live in. There are about 20,000 recognized museums in the world today and roughly a third of them are located in the United States. Most museums fall into one of three categories: art, history, or science.

Some, like the trailside museums found in state parks, are no more than tiny buildings featuring several glass cases of specimens and a few charts and diagrams. Others, such as forty-acre Mystic Seaport in Mystic, Connecticut, are rambling complexes of buildings and other artifacts representing a particular time and life-style in American history. Some museums contain general collections, including many different types of treasures. Others specialize, centering on subjects as diverse as dolls, basketball, buttons, glass, airplanes, or trolleys. There are even museums devoted to nuts, locks, and cartoons. Corporate museums tell the story of a company's history, and local museums focus on the tale of a town.

Museums get their paintings, artifacts, and specimens in several ways. Many are donated by research scientists who work for universities. Others are donated by private collectors. Still others are bought from private collectors and dealers, and at auction. Museums also sell and trade pieces to one another.

In terms of physical plant, museums vary from classical buildings with columns and graceful stairways, to modern structures with skylights and spiraling exhibit areas, to old jails or gristmills. Restored ships make great storehouses for museums about maritime history. The Cloisters museum in New York is made from sections of monasteries shipped in from France and Spain.

The first museum appeared about 2,400 years ago, when world conqueror Alexander the Great handed over to his teacher, the famous Greek philosopher Aristotle, a large amount of money and all the natural-history specimens he had collected during his travels through the lands he had conquered. The groundwork had begun for the establishment of the first museum, or "Mouseion," in Alexandria, a city in Egypt founded by the Greeks.

The Mouseion included temples, gardens, the most ambitious

library in the ancient world, and even a zoo. It also had living quarters for scholars who studied science, literature, and philosophy. Eventually the museum was destroyed. No similar museum existed until modern times. Kings and emperors assembled huge private collections in their homes, but unlike the Mouseion, these were not places for research and study. No attempts were made to identify the objects collected by rich and powerful men such as the Roman emperor Nero, who looted Greek temples and took home the booty to decorate his own home.

Today, museums play the role of the Mouseion. They educate and entertain, and they serve as places where scholars do research, learning more and more about our past.

Visiting an Art Museum

America's first art museum was launched in Philadelphia in 1784, when artist Charles Willson Peale opened a section of his home to the public in order to share his collection of paintings. The collection was later moved to Independence Hall. Today, our country has more than 700 art museums. One, Chicago's Art Institute, occupies twenty acres.

If you are like many kids, you may wonder what is so exciting about visiting an art museum. You might wonder, too, how people can stare at a single painting for such a long time. They do so for two reasons. People who are interested in technique—how the artist uses the brush to convey light and dark, the shape of the forms in the paintings, the way color is used—spend time examining the way the work has been made.

Other viewers, however, are lost in a different world. They use the paintings to spur their own imaginations. You can join them by letting your thoughts wander as you ask yourself questions about the picture in front of you.

- What is the relationship between the woman and the little girl in the picture? Is that the child's mother, her nurse, her aunt? How do they feel about each other?
- Where have they come from? Where are they getting ready to go?
- What do you think they might be saying to each other? (You might ask one of your parents to pretend to be the adult in the painting, while you take the part of the child. Make up a conversation together, playing the parts of the people in the painting.)

Why Can't We Touch the Art?

It's often tempting to run your fingers along the smooth marble of a statue or to feel the bumpy surface of an oil painting. But art museums can't allow that. Part of the reason is that objects could get broken by accident. Another, less obvious, reason is that the moisture and oils in your skin can actually cause damage to the delicate surface of an art object. Mold can develop on paintings, which damages the surface of the canvas. If everyone passing through were to fondle that splendid suit of armor, it might develop rust. Moisture, air, light, insects, and atmospheric pollutants can all cause injury. Even breathing can harm a delicate piece of art! That's why museum staffs put great thought and money into devising ways to control the air temperature and humidity in their galleries. Help them protect and preserve the artwork by respecting their rules.

Treasure Hunt

The next time you visit an art museum, take a notebook and pencil along. Go on a treasure hunt! Treasure hunts get you involved with the artwork. They give you a reason to look closely. And they help you remember what you have seen.

You might decide to see how many animals you can find (from the Greek statue of a ram to the canary singing in the cage in the Impressionist painting). Make a note of the artwork where you found each beast. If you look carefully, you'll probably find dozens.

Or try a food treasure hunt. Who's eating what, and where? You may find hunters roasting a wild boar over an open spit, a group of young people enjoying a picnic in a field filled with wildflowers, or a group of men hoisting tankards of ale in a tavern. Use your notebook to jot down a description of the setting, the foods, and the folks who are doing the eating.

Backstage at a Museum

Many different people work behind the scenes at a museum. A small museum may be run by a single person, while a major museum relies on hundreds of employees as well as dedicated volunteers. The larger the museum, the more varied the staff. Here are some of their positions and responsibilities.

The *curators* assemble and care for the collections and plan exhibits. They do research to find out more about the objects, and they sometimes give lectures and teach classes. Major museums have curators for each of their areas of specialty.

Some of the questions curators answer most frequently about the objects in their collections, whether they are baseball cards or ancient mummies, are—What is this? How was it used? How old is it? Where did it come from? How much is it worth? Curators get help from *cataloguers* and *photographers,* who assist in keeping records that describe the objects and the way in which they were acquired by the museum. *Librarians* and *editors* organize research materials and prepare guidebooks and catalogues of the exhibits.

The *conservator* is the person responsible for the preservation and restoration of items in the museum's collections. An art conservator may oversee the restoration of a painting that is cracking or fading. In a science museum, a taxidermist (someone who stuffs and mounts the skins of animals to preserve their lifelike appearance) may serve as a conservator. Curators and conservators are often supported by different types of scientists, such as paleontologists (who study fossils) and archeologists (who study the physical remains of ancient peoples). *Exhibit designers* plan the exhibits, deciding where and how to best display the artifacts. *Carpenters* and craftspeople are the skilled workers who install the display cases and cabinets and build the detailed room models, dioramas, and other exhibit spaces planned by the designers.

Security guards are stationed throughout the museum to protect the collections from theft and vandalism. They also discourage visitors from touching the objects on display. Some museums keep a guard on duty all night long, who checks in regularly with the police. Watchdogs are sometimes used as well.

Guards may be assisted in their work by elaborate electronic security systems that sound an alarm if an object is moved or if a

particular barrier is crossed. Closed-circuit TV cameras are used to keep an eye on the galleries while other devices register unusual sounds, motions, or vibrations within the building. Some museums even have a centralized control console where the operator can contact any guard at any time (remember, some museums are bigger than a city block) and automatically close doors anywhere within the museum complex.

Depending upon size, a museum may have a *building superintendent* and *custodians* to maintain the grounds and buildings, staff for the cafeteria and gift shop, and tour guides who introduce visitors to the museum.

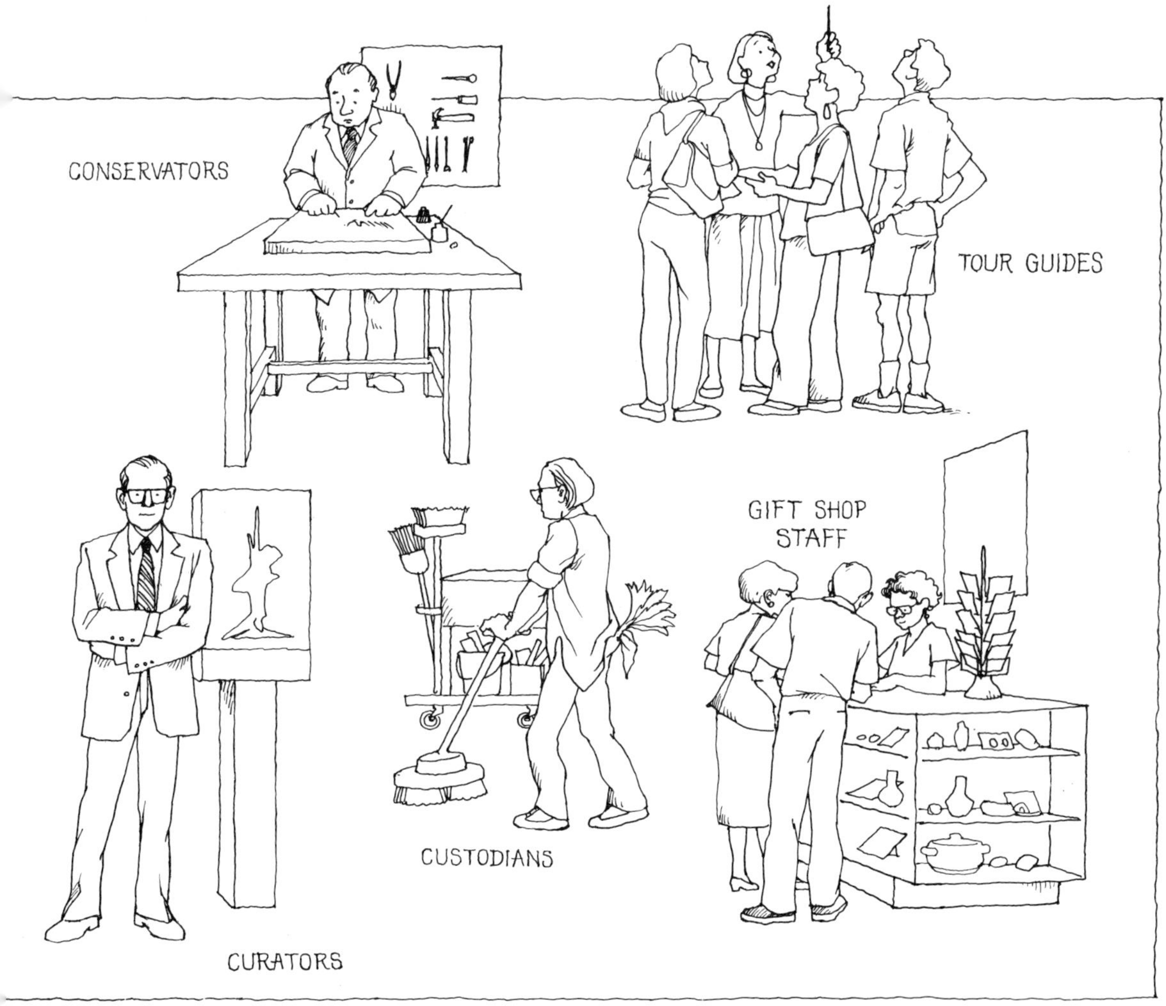

Is It the Real Thing?

How does a museum tell a genuine artifact from a fake? Can anyone tell just by looking?

Absolutely not. Skillful craftspeople have produced forgeries of works by famous artists that are so accurate that only scientific testing can distinguish them from the originals. To determine the authenticity of a painting, experts examine the picture under ultraviolet and infrared light, which allows them to see if the surface of the picture has been repaired, repainted, or in any way changed. Paintings can also be X-rayed. A microbeam, a hypodermic needle the width of a human hair, can be inserted into the surface of a painting. When withdrawn, the needle contains samples of all the layers of paint and varnish on the canvas, which can provide lots of information. (What do you think the evidence points to if there's a layer of paint underneath that dates back a hundred years, and the painting is being presented as a work by a painter who lived two hundred years ago?)

When it comes to separating a genuine dinosaur bone from a fake one, scientists often resort to a procedure known as carbon 14 dating. Animals and plants all absorb tiny amounts of C-14 (a radioactive form of carbon) during their lives. When an organism dies, it no longer absorbs C-14, and the radioactivity level within the organism begins to lessen. By measuring the amount of radioactivity remaining, scientists can estimate how long ago the plant or animal died. This process can also be used to determine the age of cloth made from cotton, wool, or other natural fibers, and of artifacts made from wood.

SIX

Two Special Kinds of Parks

At first glance, zoological parks and amusement parks don't have much in common. The first is full of live animals, while the second is full of machines. One emphasizes education, while the other stresses plain old fun. But look below the surface a bit. From the point of view of a tourist, the two types of parks have a strong similarity. Both are popular family attractions, the type of attractions that have something for everyone. Learning a little about their history and their plans for the future can make your visit an even richer experience.

Who Invented Amusement Parks?

Amusement parks were originally built for adults, not children. In the early 1900s, the trolley became an important means of public transportation. Powered by electricity, trolley cars traveled along a track, carrying riders between home and work. The power companies often charged the trolley owners a flat monthly fee for the electricity used to move the cars. Since most people rode the trolleys only to get to their jobs, the owners needed to find a way to boost their earnings by giving people a reason to ride them on Saturdays and Sundays. To lure weekend riders, they decided to build recreational facilities at the ends of the trolley lines. This practice began in New England and spread across the country.

In the beginning, the facilities were very simple. People climbed aboard the trolley to get to a pretty picnic grove for a weekend outing. Sometimes the trolley companies also provided concerts at the end of the line. Pleased by the success of their plan, some companies added an amusement ride, usually a merry-go-round or Ferris wheel. Lake Compounce in Bristol, Connecticut, the oldest park in the country that is still in continuous operation under the same management, began in 1846 as the brainchild of a trolley company.

Amusement Parks Today

Amusement parks continue to do a booming business today. Attendance at U.S. parks hit a record-breaking 249 million visits in 1988, with gross receipts of over $4 billion. The parks provide over a quarter of a million summer jobs each year, and about two-thirds of these are filled by young people between the ages of fourteen and nineteen. They sell tickets and souvenirs, operate games and rides, prepare and sell food, do maintenance work, and serve as lifeguards and entertainers.

Eager to keep visitors coming back, amusement-park owners are always on the lookout for fresh attractions that are safe and easy to maintain and that occupy a limited amount of space (land is expensive). A recent advance in this area is the ride simulator, which is described as a theater that moves. Riders enter the simulator and take a seat for an exciting adventure. Film, sound, motion, wind, and other special effects are used to create the feel of experiences such as careening down an Olympic bobsled run or flying a jet plane.

Compared to other rides, which can cost up to $6 million, simulators are inexpensive, with prices starting at about $115,000. Small ones handle several hundred riders per hour, while large ones can accommodate several thousand. They are so compact and portable that they can even be set up inside a shopping mall, providing extra revenues in parts of the country where amusement parks close down for the winter. Safe and easy to maintain, simulators are destined to become increasingly popular in the coming years. Sophisticated animation techniques and 3-D projection effects are other examples of high-tech wizardry that are becoming regular parts of the amusement-park scene.

Despite the invention of dozens of flashy new attractions, traditional standbys such as the merry-go-round, Ferris wheel, and roller coaster continue to be among the most popular attractions. The largest merry-go-rounds ever made featured horses standing six abreast and could hold over a hundred riders. They were manufactured by the firm of Stein & Goldstein in Brooklyn, N.Y. Unfortunately, not one of these models is known to have survived. Hand-carved, hand-painted horses have been replaced by cast aluminum ones, and instead of old-time organs, the music comes from stereo systems. Yet there's still an old-fashioned feeling about riding a merry-go-round.

Some parks still have authentic antique carousels with wooden animals. Continental European carousels and American ones move in a counterclockwise direction. On British carousels, the horses travel clockwise. The old horses usually have only one fancy or "show" side, complete with jeweled harness and ornate carvings. The other side is almost plain, and the effect would be spoiled if the horses were switched to go in the opposite direction from the way they were originally intended to face.

Gustav Dentzel, most famous of the American merry-go-round makers, built a two-story version in 1890. The double-decker turned out to be unprofitable, however. It took too long to load and unload passengers, reducing the number of tickets that could be sold per hour. Another version of the merry-go-round, one that fared better, was the flying horses. Instead of being mounted on a platform below, the flying horses hung from individual rods suspended from a frame overhead. The famous flying horses at Watch Hill, R.I., continue to entertain riders today. Currently operated by electricity, they were first powered by hand, then by horse, and then by water. The flying horses have evolved into a whole series of popular modern flying machines found in amusement parks across the country.

For scary rides, roller coasters still top the list. Modern coasters are chock-full of sophisticated safety features and are virtually accident-free, but that doesn't mean they are any less frightening. Cars clank up to the top of the track, where the fear of falling off is often increased by the lack of railings. With strategically placed high-speed stretches and curves and dramatic drops, roller coasters create fear based on the illusion of danger.

Roller coasters trace their roots to the early Russian ice slides. A Frenchman tried to import that idea to Paris near the end of the eighteenth century, but the weather was too warm. Instead, he built a ramp made up of rollers, which a toboggan could slide down. This ramp was the early ancestor of the modern roller coaster.

Ferris wheels evolved from amusement devices called "pleasure wheels," which had a long history in Europe and the Orient.

The first one built in America was Charles D. Dare's twenty-foot-high wooden Dare Wheel, produced in Brooklyn, N.Y., in 1870. By the late 1800s, metal tubing had replaced the wooden frames. The granddaddy of today's amusement park Ferris wheels was the 264-foot-high wheel built by George W. G. Ferris for the 1893 Columbia Exposition at Chicago. It was taller than some thirty-story skyscrapers. Each of its thirty-six cars held sixty people, which meant that, fully loaded, it held 2,160 passengers. It was not a ride to take if you were in a rush, since it took about an hour to load the giant wheel and each complete revolution took twenty minutes, with two nonstop revolutions making up each turn. How much time would you have to allow if you wanted to take a ride?

Today, some rides are bought new from manufacturers, while

others are purchased from parks that have closed or where they are no longer popular. Advertisements in a recent issue of *Funworld,* the colorful magazine published by the International Association of Amusement Parks and Attractions, offered a 1987 portable giant Ferris wheel, ninety feet high with twenty-one passenger cars, for $350,000, and a used sky tram (a cable car ride) for just $50,000.

Some rides, like the new roller coaster that opened in Kansas City's Worlds of Fun in 1989, are custom made for a particular park. "Timber Wolf" can carry 1,200 passengers per hour on its two-and-a-half-minute ride. It took a crew of forty workers several months to assemble the giant wooden coaster, which includes fifteen tons of nails, 80,000 bolts, and 680,000 board feet of lumber. From the coaster's highest point, a hundred feet above the ground, passengers plummet ninety-five feet earthward at a speed of fifty-three miles per hour. The park's general manager describes the ride as "two and a half minutes of out-of-control, breathless terror."

Where Do Zoos Get Their Animals?

Zoos got their start in the form of animal collections kept by the ancient Egyptians and Chinese, the Greeks and the Romans, for the pleasure of the nobility. Most of the animals were taken from the wild. By the early 1800s, when zoos were first established in the United States, many species had already been overcollected, endangering their future. At that time, animal hunters traveled to distant corners of the world to capture exotic animals. These costly, time-consuming, and often dangerous expeditions also provided the opportunity to gather information about animals and their natural environment.

AN EGYPTIAN WALL PAINTING SHOWING MENAGERIE ANIMALS

THE ZOO AT VERSAILLES, FRANCE, IN THE 1600s

THE PHILADELPHIA ZOO-1879

GERMAN ANIMAL DEALER CARL HAGENBECK OPENED THE FIRST ZOO WITHOUT CAGES IN 1907.

The earliest animal dealers were men who worked near the docks in busy port cities. They were often able to buy rare birds and other animals from sailors returning from distant parts of the globe. Other animals were obtained from animal handlers or hunters, who captured the animals in the wild.

Today, fewer than 1 percent of the animals taken from the wild go to zoos and aquariums. It is, in fact, illegal to import certain species into the United States. Most of the animals now on display in American zoos and aquariums were born in captivity. Half of those have parents who were also born in captivity.

Sometimes zoos receive animals as gifts. Premier Chou En-lai presented former President Richard Nixon with a pair of rare pandas. Gifts from the people of China to the people of the United States, Ling-Ling (means "cute little girl") and Hsing-Hsing (means "new") were sent to live in the National Zoo in Washington, D.C.

Zoos also get animals by trading with other zoos, both in this country and around the world. Sometimes the trades are simple exchanges, like trading your baseball card doubles, but some are more complex. Some years ago the Bronx Zoo in New York wanted to obtain a male takin, a goatlike mammal with a golden coat and horns that point backward. The takin comes from the Himalayas, the high mountains of Burma and China. Because its meat is considered a delicacy, so many of the animals have been killed that they have become quite rare. The Bronx Zoo already had a female and wanted to get a male so that they could try to breed the two and help save the species.

The zoo contacted Frederik J. Zeehadelaar, one of the most notable wild-animal suppliers in the world. Zeehadelaar knew of only one available male takin, and it lived in a zoo in Rangoon, Burma. The Rangoon Zoo wanted other animals in exchange for its takin. Eventually, the zoo agreed to accept two giraffes and four zebras. But because the Bronx Zoo did not have the appropriate animals to exchange, Zeehadelaar had to purchase the giraffes and zebras for them and then deliver them to the Rangoon Zoo before arranging shipment of the takin to New York.

Zoos also acquire animals by breeding them in captivity, as was the plan for the takin. Because so many exotic animals are in danger of extinction, scientists, veterinarians, and animal handlers are hard at work trying to discover ways of improving the likelihood that animals from other parts of the world will reproduce in our zoos.

What Do the Animals Eat?

The kitchen in a zoo is called a commissary. This is where the food is stored and prepared. A large zoo may require over 50,000 pounds of meat and 20,000 pounds of fish each year, in addition to hundreds of tons of fruit, grain, and vegetables. The shopping list includes ground horsemeat, beef, and chicken for the big cats, processed grains for the hoofed animals such as zebras and antelope, live crickets for lizards and some types of birds, live mice, chickens, and other small mammals for the snakes and alligators, and fish and clams for the penguins, sea lions, and porpoises. A full-grown African elephant feasts on 125 to 150 pounds of food a day, including hay, grain mash, vegetables, and fruit, washed down by about fifty gallons of water. The great apes and monkeys thrive on salads, as do many species of birds.

Birds are a zoo's choosiest eaters and tend to require the greatest variety of ingredients. The bird commissary at the National Zoo in Washington, D.C., has 150 color-coded menu cards that keep track of which foods each kind of bird eats, the quantity, and in what form. A single palm cockatoo receives a prettily prepared breakfast tray bearing two string beans, a chunk of coconut, four slices of carrot, two pieces of corn on the cob, four pieces each of orange and apple, two monkey biscuits, two tablespoons of bird-of-prey diet (a mixture of meat and fish with feathers and bones ground up in it), one tablespoon of bread and milk mixture, three-fourths of a cup of sunflower seeds, two small peanut-butter sandwiches, a couple of kale leaves, and some chopped greens.

Other birds thrive on diets that vary from frozen mice and rats to live Canadian nightcrawlers, hardboiled eggs to whole butterfish. Among the most discriminating eaters are the tawny frog-mouth owls, who insist on live mice, hand fed to them by their keeper.

What Are Endangered Species?

Endangered species are kinds of animals that are at risk of extinction, of dying out of existence. From 1800 to 1900, one species of animal became extinct every eighteen months. From 1900 to the present, species are disappearing at the rate of one every year. The global extinction rate for wildlife today is about fifty time faster than it was during the age of dinosaurs. At the current rate, two species of birds become extinct every three years. By the year 2000, that rate is expected to increase to one species per year.

The major cause of endangered species is habitat destruction. A habitat is the place where an animal lives in the wild. Examples include rolling grasslands, frozen arctic tundra, rain forest, and desert. Between 1961 and 1987, the world's population doubled. As the population has grown, people have cut down forests, cultivated grasslands, and flooded plains to meet their need to grow food and build homes. In the process, many natural habitats have been destroyed.

Zoos and acquariums are striving to give animals and fish living conditions that are more like their natural habitats. The ideal naturalistic habitat provides the animal with food, protection from its enemies, shelter from the elements or extremes in temperature, and conditions that are right for bearing young. For some animals, that might mean trees (for birds that require perches) or pools (for rhinos to bathe in). The sea lion needs an artificial sea, along with islands for sunbathing. The giant anaconda, a South American snake that can grow to thirty feet, needs a river bank or swamp setting with lots of logs and tree branches for curling and climbing. In a naturalistic setting, animals are more likely to stay healthy and to breed, perpetuating their species.

In designing the right setting, zoo staffers need to carefully consider animal behavior. They need to protect people from the animals, so they take into account the fact that a leopard that can leap twelve feet needs to be separated from viewers by more than a narrow moat. They also need to protect the animals from visitors

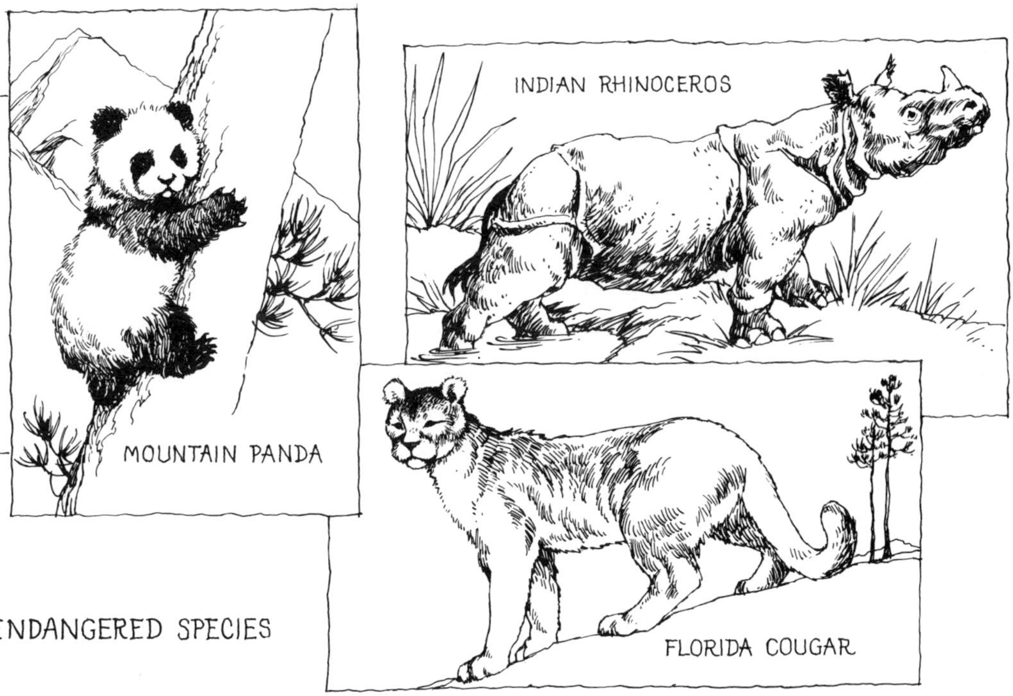

SOME ENDANGERED SPECIES

who might harm them by tossing into their homes everything from candy and rubber balls to sticks and stones.

Over 112 million people visit zoos and aquariums in the United States and Canada each year, more than the total number who attend football, hockey, and baseball games combined. In earlier days the main purpose of the zoos was to educate and entertain by introducing people to exotic animals they might otherwise never see. Today, the zoos have another important purpose. They are trying to save endangered species. As they become increasingly successful at breeding animals in captivity, they also work at reintroducing endangered animals to protected natural habitats. Early successes include the return of captive-born golden lion tamarins to Brazil and Arabian oryx to Oman.

Design Your Own Zoo Exhibit

Choose an animal to study in depth. When you visit a zoo or aquarium, read the signs, observe your animal, and talk to the keeper. What kind of habitat does the zoo provide? Does your animal tend to be a loner or does it mix with others? Is it a carnivore (meat eater), omnivore (eater of both meat and plants), or herbivore (plant eater)? Is it nocturnal (awake and active at night) or diurnal (awake and active in the day)? Does it need things to climb on, crawl under, swim in, hide behind? How much space does it require? Make sketches and notes so that you'll remember all the information when you get home. If possible, purchase miniatures of your animal at the museum shop.

When you get home, make a detailed plan or drawing, showing the features your animal needs in an ideal zoo setting. Refer to your notes and sketches for ideas and information. Then build a model enclosure, using a piece of scrap wood as a base. Use plasticene to anchor "trees" made from twigs. Make caves from rocks or clay or by holding rocks together with plasticene. Use your imagination to create moats, islands, fencing, and pools (shallow dishes of water or fakes made of aluminum foil, perhaps). Be sure to create "food" for your animal. Bits of straw for hay, tiny plastic bananas, bits of cereal for grain, and so on. When you finish your exhibit, move your miniatures in and add a sign identifying and describing the animals.

If you really enjoy learning about exotic animals, you might want to expand your collection of exhibits, specializing in a different species each time you visit a zoo. The more you know about the animals, the better you will be at creating the perfect zoo environment for them. You may even decide to build a complete zoo of your own, inventing displays and duplicating particularly good ones you've seen.

SEVEN

At the Seashore

The seashore is a wonderful place to swim, fly kites, play Frisbee, and build sandcastles. Take some time, too, to lie in the sun with your eyes closed, listening to the sounds of the water lapping the shore, the gulls cawing overhead. Can you smell the seaweed and the salty air? How is this beach different from the last beach you visited? How is it the same? What makes a beach extra special for you?

Where Did All the Sand Come From?

Sand is made from the action of wind and water on rock. Sometimes sand is transported by rivers and by heavy rains from inland regions. Each time the tide comes in or goes out and each time there is a storm, the sand shifts and the face of the beach changes.

The texture and color of the sand varies tremendously, depending upon the materials it is made of and the nature of the currents and waves at the particular beach. Most beach sand is made from crushed quartz, a mineral that is found in just about every kind of rock. It makes a grayish beach. Sand that is nearly black contains large amounts of pulverized volcanic rock. Sand that is soft and chalky, like that found in the Florida Keys, usually contains a high amount of ground-up shells and coral. Still other beaches are made of yellow, greenish, pale purple, or reddish sand.

Sand dunes develop when very high tides toss the sand high on the shore and then the winds carry it even higher. If there is no coastal cliff to block it, the sand forms hills that sometimes grow to fifty feet or more in height. Like a glacier, a live sand dune (one that is still forming and growing) creeps inland slowly but steadily, engulfing bushes, trees, and other beach vegetation that happen to be in its path.

If you have the chance to visit different beaches frequently, consider collecting sand samples. Take along a supply of plastic bags and twist ties for storage. Take some masking tape too, so you can label each bag according to the location where you found it. (If you want to expand your collection, add soil samples from other places you visit, labeling each addition carefully.) At home, spread out bits of each sample and examine them with a magnifying glass to get a sense of just how varied they are in color and texture.

Beach Mosaic

A mosaic is a design made up of many small pieces. To make a beach mosaic, collect some small, interesting pebbles and shells. At home, rub them with mineral oil to make them look satiny. Then take a flat piece of wood (such as a scrap of board or plywood) and draw a simple design on it with a pencil. Use the pebbles to fill up areas of your design, rearranging them until you like it. Then pick them up one by one and dab a drop of white glue on the board, gluing each one in place, or spread the glue over a small area (1 inch square) and glue down pebbles and shells until the area is covered before moving on to the next one.

If there are large areas that you want to use as background, consider covering them with a layer of sand. Mix white glue with an equal amount of water and apply it to the background with a paintbrush. Sprinkle sand over it until the glue is completely covered. When you finish, let your work dry. Then add a picture hook and it's ready to hang, a reminder of your trips to the seashore.

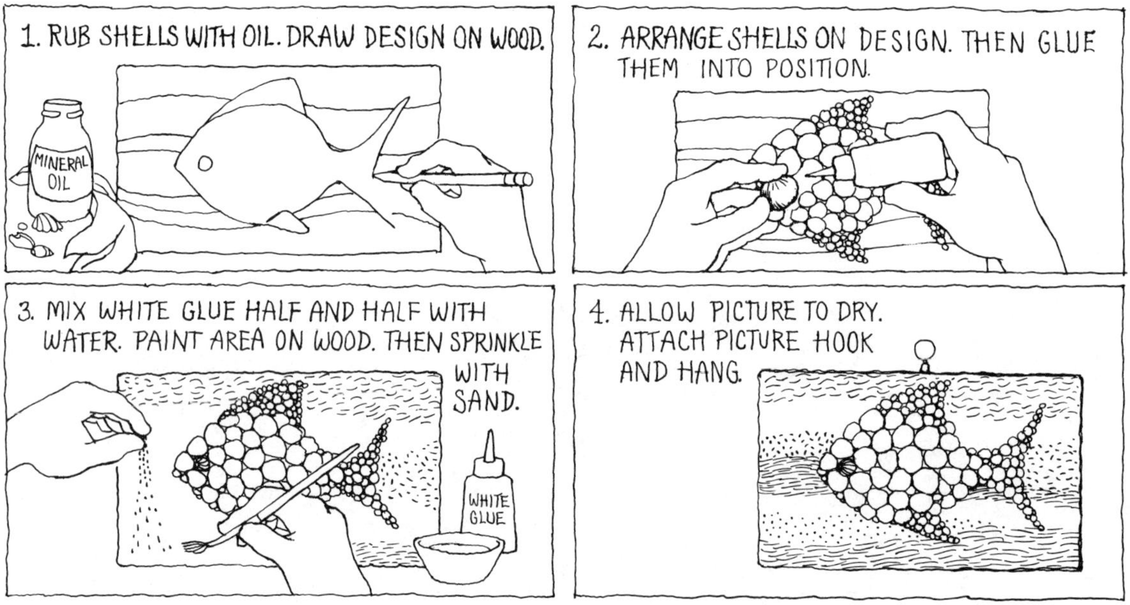

Where Does the Water Go When the Tide Goes Out?

The water doesn't actually go anywhere when the tide goes out. As the earth rotates, each section of the sea lines up with the "attractive force" or pull of the moon. Have you ever watched a wave roll in? Often it reaches the shore at one end of the beach a few seconds before it crashes against the sand at the other end. The tide is actually a great wave that travels through the ocean, reaching one point on the coastline earlier than another. On the Atlantic coast, the wave moves from south to north, which is why the times of high and low tides become later as one travels from Florida to Nova Scotia. What actually happens is that the level of the water rises and falls as the tidal wave passes through it.

Tidal patterns differ according to how the shore lines up with the moon's pull. On the Atlantic coast, the tide rises and falls twice a day, which is also true of most of the Pacific coast. (The Gulf of Mexico, however, has only one tide a day.) If the moon remained in a fixed position relative to the earth, high and low tide in a given place would occur at the same times each day. But that is not the situation. The moon rotates around the earth in a cycle that takes about twenty-nine days. This means that it reaches a set position about fifty minutes later each day. As a result, each morning high tide is about fifty minutes later than the one the previous day, and each afternoon high tide occurs about fifty minutes later than the afternoon high the day before. Absolute high tide and absolute low tide occur about six hours apart.

When you plan to spend time at the seashore, keeping track of the tides is helpful because some activities are better suited for different tides. High tide is often preferred for swimming. At low tide, you may have to walk far, far from the shore to get to water deep enough to swim in. Also, the water at many beaches seems cleaner when the tide is "in," or high.

Low tide, on the other hand, is the most rewarding time to collect or observe marine life. The days immediately following a full moon, when the tides are at their lowest, are best. The lower the tide, the richer the marine life revealed in the pools left exposed in the rocks and sand by an outbound sea. Low tide is also good for clamming, and the hard-packed wet sand left behind when the tide goes out is fine for jogging, too.

Collecting Seashells

People wear their skeletons beneath their skin, but there are other animals that carry their skeletons on the outside of their bodies. Some of these are the clam, scallop, snail, and oyster. These animals are called mollusks, and the part of them that we call a shell is actually their skeleton, or supporting framework. Shells are made from lime, which the animal gets from the food it eats and the water it drinks. Lime is also used in the formation of human skeletons.

Mollusks that have a single shell, such as snails and whelks, are called univalves. Others, such as mussels and clams, have two shells and are called bivalves. It is always important to remember that a seashell is or was the covering of a live animal. This covering protects the animal from others that might wish to eat it.

The empty shells that you find on the beach are called dead shells. They tend to be chipped or broken, and if they have been exposed to the sun for a long time, their colors may have faded.

Although the seashore is the most popular spot for shell collecting, you can also find specimens near lakes, streams, and ponds. There are freshwater mollusks as well as saltwater ones, and there are even some that live out of water, such as the land snails that can be found in damp, forest areas.

When you go shell collecting, take along a plastic bucket or a heavy plastic bag. Be certain to check carefully around piers and pilings and old boats or other pieces of debris. Tide pools and clusters of rock that stick out of the water only at low tide are also good places to search.

Once you have cleaned your treasures, you need to identify them. You will need a shell handbook or field guide, preferably one that has lots of color illustrations and that specializes in the region of the country where you have done your collecting. In the handbook, shells will probably be identified by both scientific name and common name. *Littorina littorea* is the scientific name for the common periwinkle found along the northern Atlantic coast; *Chlamys hericus* refers to the pink scallop that lives along the Pacific coast. Match each of your shells with the picture it most closely resembles, paying special attention to size, coloring, and distinctive markings. Make a label for each of your specimens, listing its scientific and common names along with the date and location of the find.

You can store your shells in a divided box, like the kind Christmas ornaments come in, or an egg carton. Glue each label to the corresponding compartment, or prepare a key and tape it to the top of the box. If you want to display your shells on the wall, use white glue to attach them to a piece of wood, fiberboard, or even heavy cardboard if they are not too large. To make them look silky, rub them with mineral oil before mounting. Attach a picture hanger to the back and you're ready to hang up your collection.

Amazing Seaweed

You can find seaweed on just about any saltwater beach you visit, but the type of seaweed will vary with the location of the beach. Sea lettuce (ulva) thrives on the Atlantic, Pacific, and Gulf coasts, while giant kelp (macrocystis) is found only on the Pacific coast, and Irish moss sticks to the North Atlantic area. Seaweed comes in a broad spectrum of colors, including many variations of green, brown, and red as well as shades of yellow, purple, and blue. Members of the algae family, seaweeds are plants that grow in water and contain chlorophyll, but have no roots or flowers.

Seaweed is very useful stuff. It provides food and shelter for many marine creatures, and certain types of birds use it in building their nests. Seaweed makes excellent fertilizer, and many types have high nutritional value. If you would like to experiment with edible seaweeds, you can add some bright green sea lettuce *(ulva lactuca)* to your dinner salad. Harvest your sea lettuce, which is easy to find because it looks like limp salad lettuce, in the water. Take it home in a bucket of seawater to keep it fresh. Rinse it with tap water and shred it. It doesn't have much taste, but its lovely color has lots of eye appeal.

Irish moss is used to thicken puddings. Why not try making some Irish Moss Pudding yourself? (See page 72.)

Collecting Seaweed

Lots of people collect shells. For a more out-of-the-ordinary collection, try seaweed. You'll find specimens at nearly every beach, particularly if you check around rocks and pilings and in the grasses that tend to grow near the shoreline. Some types are free-floating, while others use holdfasts (which look like tiny suction cups) to root themselves to a solid object, such as a rock. With the latter, try using the sharp edge of a seashell to pry the specimen loose without damaging the holdfast.

Seaweed discolors quickly in fresh water, so it is wise to bring along a container with a tight top so that you can carry your specimens home in seawater. As you find specimens on the beach, place them in a bucket of seawater, rinsing carefully to remove sand. Then put them in your container for the trip home.

To preserve your specimens, you will need to press them. Pour parts of the seawater into a shallow pan and float one specimen in it. Then slide a sheet of stiff paper under it and lift it out of the water. Gently arrange it exactly the way you want it to be preserved. Put the wet paper with the specimen on it on top of a few sheets of newspaper. Then cover the seaweed with a thick pad of paper towels. Put a board on top and weight it down with books or rocks. Change the newspaper and the paper towels the next day, never removing the seaweed from the paper. Continue this procedure for several days, until the specimen is completely dried out.

If you are preserving several specimens at once, you can layer them on top of each other, with pads of paper towels in between and each specimen mounted on its own sheet of paper. That way you can weight them all down together. If you want to preserve one of the slimy, gelatinous seaweeds, let it sit in the air until partially dry before beginning the pressing process.

The specimens will probably glue themselves to the sheets of paper during pressing, but if they don't, secure them with a little rubber cement. Mount the pages in a scrapbook, being certain to label each specimen with its name along with the date you found it and the location of the find. Your library will have a field guide you can use to help with identification.

Irish Moss Pudding

You will need: cheesecloth and a double boiler, ½ cup of Irish moss cut into small pieces, one quart of milk, ⅜ cup of sugar, ½ teaspoon of vanilla, and some salt and nutmeg.

1. Make a crude bag out of the cheesecloth and put the Irish moss into it.
2. Put one quart of milk into the top of the double boiler, with boiling water in the bottom part. Put the bag of seaweed in the milk and cook for half an hour.
3. Squeeze the bag often by pressing it with a wooden spoon.
4. After half an hour, add the sugar, the vanilla, a pinch of salt, and, if you like, a pinch of nutmeg.
5. Pour the mixture into pudding cups and chill. Discard cheesecloth bag.

Makes 8 half-cup servings.

EIGHT

The Big City Scene

The major fact about cities is that they are very densely populated compared to suburban and rural or country areas. Many more people live on each square acre of land in the city than in the country. Because there is less of it and more people who need to use it, land in the city tends to be very expensive. In order to use every possible bit of space and to provide places for all of the people to live and work, cities don't just grow outward. They expand downward and upward as well, making use of space below and above the ground. The next time you visit a big city, try to imagine what is happening high above your head and far below your feet right at the moment when you are strolling along the sidewalk.

Why Are Skyscrapers Built?

Skyscrapers, formally defined as buildings over twenty stories high, are built in places where vacant land is so rare and costly that it becomes necessary to build upward rather than outward. Skyscrapers allow businesspeople to get the maximum floor space for their land investment, by stacking one story on top of another, up and up. The taller the building, the greater the rentable floor space.

New developments in the quality of steel, combined with architectural advances and more powerful elevators, encouraged the construction of nearly 200 skyscrapers in New York City between 1902 and 1929, the year when a group of ambitious businesspeople decided to create the tallest building in the world. The 1,050-foot-tall Empire State Building was completed, amazingly, in less than eighteen months. Sometimes the work moved along so quickly that the steel framework rose skyward at the rate of four and a half stories a week.

The lower eighty-five floors, served by sixty-seven elevators, were crowned by a 200-foot, seventeen-story mast, making the Empire State Building far taller than its closest rival, the seventy-seven-story Chrysler Building. The mast was originally constructed as a mooring for dirigibles, large cylindrical aircraft often called blimps. During the 1920s, people thought dirigibles offered promise as an important means of transatlantic transportation, but they fell into disfavor after a number of accidents.

Like many skyscrapers, the Empire State Building gets narrower as it gets higher. It's built in layers, a bit like a giant wedding cake. It narrows at the sixth floor, then at the twenty-first, the twenty-fifth, and the thirtieth floors. From there it remains the same dimensions until the seventy-second. New layers begin again at the eighty-first and eighty-fifth floors, and then fairly regularly from there up to the hundred-and-second floor.

Local zoning laws, rules designed to protect the quality of life of people who live and work in the city, directly affected the shape of the building. The laws are written to ensure that adequate amounts of light and air can reach the ground. For example, the zoning laws decreed that any floor beyond the thirtieth could be no more than 25 percent of the area of the building site. Without zoning laws, huge rows of skyscrapers could have been built side by side, forming towering stone walls and making the city dark and stuffy.

Construction Checklist

If you visit a large city, you are almost certain to see major construction work in progress. In addition to new buildings going up, you might also see demolition work, the process by which old buildings are dismantled. In still other projects, the construction involves refurbishing an existing building to serve a different purpose. An office building, for example, might be renovated into condominiums.

Here is a checklist of construction equipment and architectural features to look for the next time you take a walk in a big city. See how many you can spot, and add others to the list as you discover them.

Structural Skeleton: Just as your bones form the skeleton that supports your body, a steel framework forms the skeleton that supports the floors and walls of a building.

Sidewalk Shed: A safety measure, the sidewalk shed is a temporary roof built over the sidewalk to protect pedestrians from debris that might fall from the construction work going on above.

Rubble Chute: Look for an enclosed tube that carries construction rubble or debris from the upper parts of the building down to the street, where it can be trucked away.

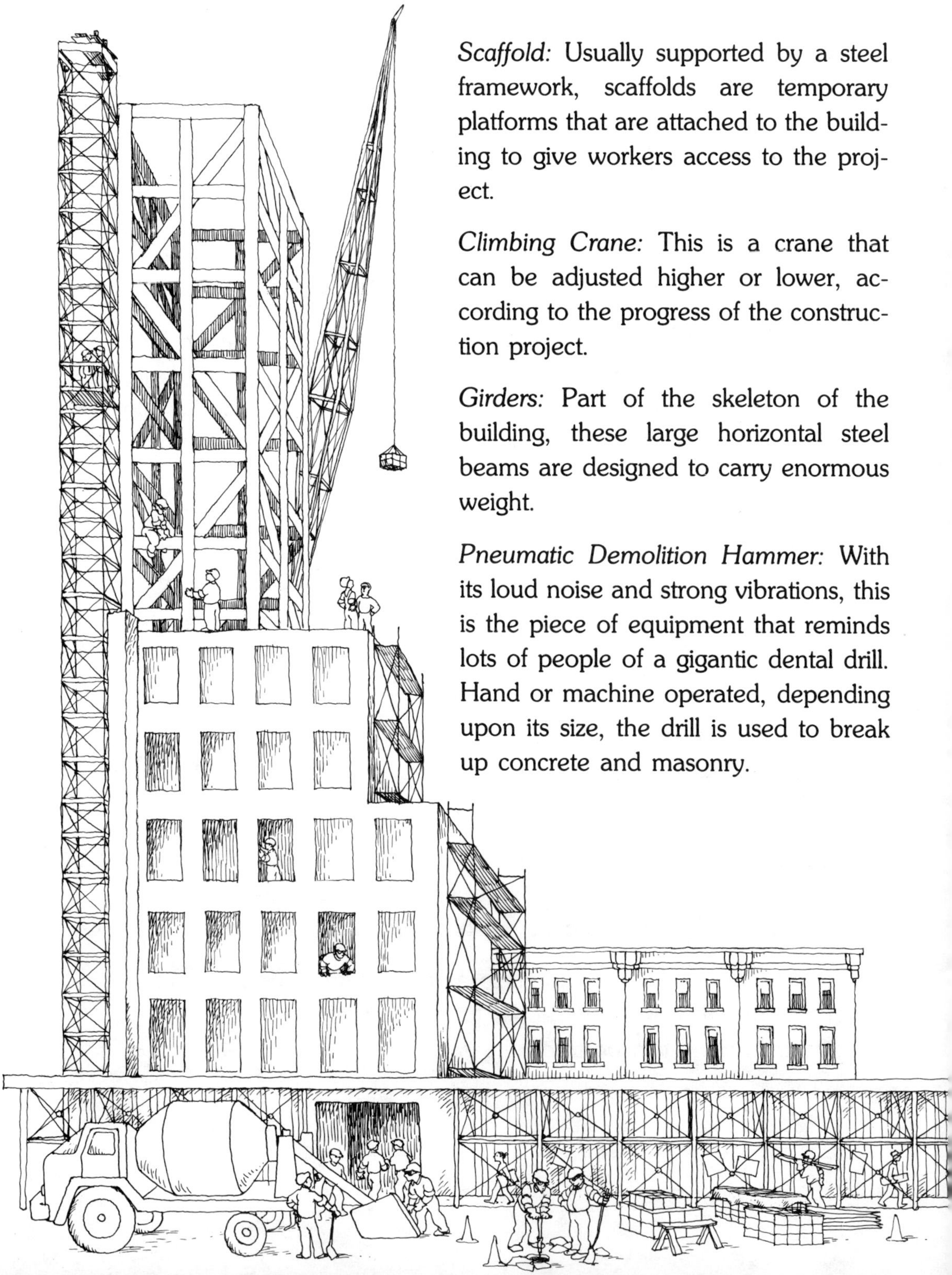

Scaffold: Usually supported by a steel framework, scaffolds are temporary platforms that are attached to the building to give workers access to the project.

Climbing Crane: This is a crane that can be adjusted higher or lower, according to the progress of the construction project.

Girders: Part of the skeleton of the building, these large horizontal steel beams are designed to carry enormous weight.

Pneumatic Demolition Hammer: With its loud noise and strong vibrations, this is the piece of equipment that reminds lots of people of a gigantic dental drill. Hand or machine operated, depending upon its size, the drill is used to break up concrete and masonry.

Setback: This is the place where the building gets narrower. It looks like a step or break (or new layer of cake) in the face of the building. Zoning laws usually require setbacks at certain height intervals.

Hard Hats and Safety Goggles: Look for construction workers wearing protective headgear and eyegear to prevent injury on the job.

A Few Words about Subways

A subway system is an underground transportation network designed to reduce the traffic above ground and to provide swift passenger transportation in crowded urban areas. Streetcars and elevated railways constructed above the city's streets were the favorite forms of urban transportation until the turn of the century, when subways became a reality. Boston was the first city in the United States to build a subway system. The one-and-a-half-mile-long track, served by electric trolley cars, was completed in 1897. New York was quick to see its advantages.

American tycoon Russell Sage responded to the first proposal to build an underground transit system in New York City by saying, "The people of New York will never go into a hole in the ground to ride." How wrong he was! By the time he died in 1906, there was already a subway running through a tunnel in Manhattan.

That doesn't mean that everyone greeted subway construction with enthusiasm. Property owners feared that their buildings would collapse, and many citizens worried that the city's underground pipes would be destroyed. Despite the opposition, by 1904 the first line was in operation. Today, nearly 2 billion New Yorkers ride the subway each year, avoiding the traffic above the ground in their efforts to get where they need to go as quickly as they can.

The basic construction method for a subway system is called "cut and cover." A trench is dug in the street. Huge vertical steel supports called soldier beams are driven into the ground around the site before the actual digging or excavation work begins. Horizontal boards are slid between the beams, forming a retaining wall. Heavy steel beams that span the trench are set on top of each pair of soldier beams, and a layer of steel plates is installed on top of these, forming a temporary road. All this takes place before the dirt is removed from the trench. Eventually, tracks are installed on the floor of the trench and the street is reconstructed above it.

There is a second type of tunnel that is used to house tracks beneath existing buildings, under rivers, and in other places where it would be impossible to dig up the surface as required in the cut and cover method. The deep-bored tunnel is made by digging vertical shafts that descend from the surface to far below the ground. The shafts, which are lined with steel to prevent them from caving in, are dug at intervals, and a tunnel is constructed between them. The shafts give workers a way of getting themselves and their ma-

"CUT AND COVER" CONSTRUCTION

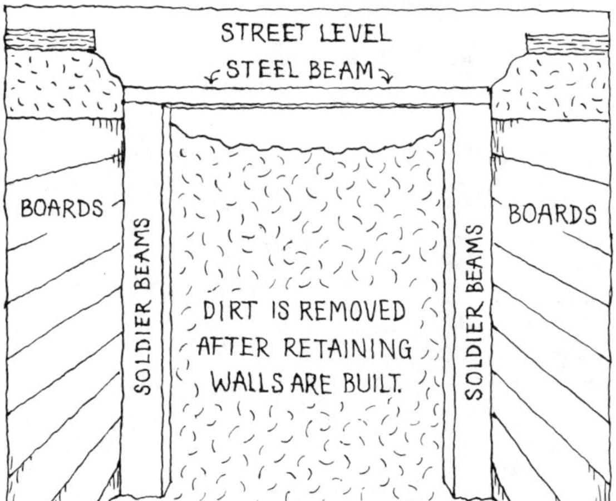

DEEP-BORED TUNNEL CONSTRUCTION

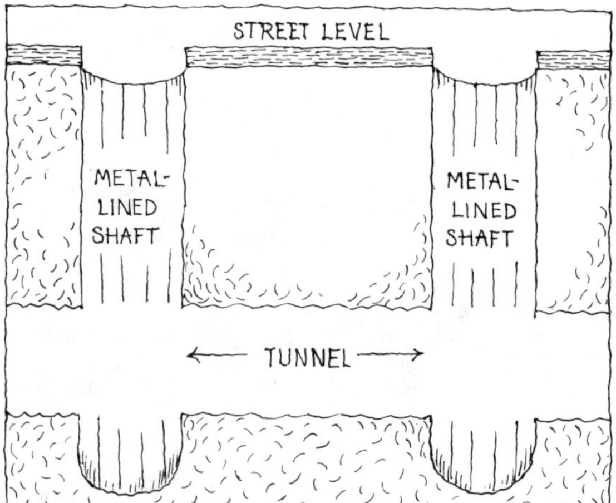

terials to the work area. They also provide fresh air to men working far beneath the earth's surface, as well as providing a means of removing the rock and soil. Powerful drills and boring machines are used to chip away the tunnel, connecting the shafts. Sometimes explosives are used to blast away at rocky areas. As each section is completed, the tracks are laid.

What's under a Manhole Cover?

As you walk through a big city, you will see lots of round steel manhole covers beneath your feet. A manhole is actually a small room located beneath the street. Manholes provide access to the many pipes, valves, transformers, cables, ducts, and meters used in the city's water, sewage, electrical, gas, and telephone systems. They provide workers with a way of getting to trouble spots and taking care of problems and maintenance chores. Large manholes are called vaults.

The next time you see a man with a protective hard hat disappear into a manhole, take a look around the site. Check out any

IN A TELEPHONE COMPANY MANHOLE

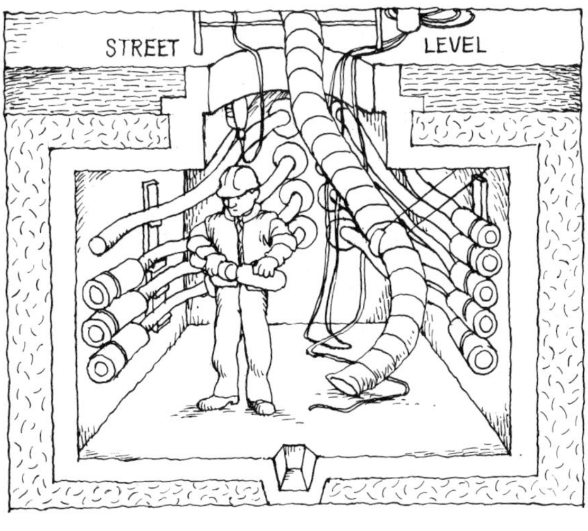

AN ELECTRIC POWER MANHOLE

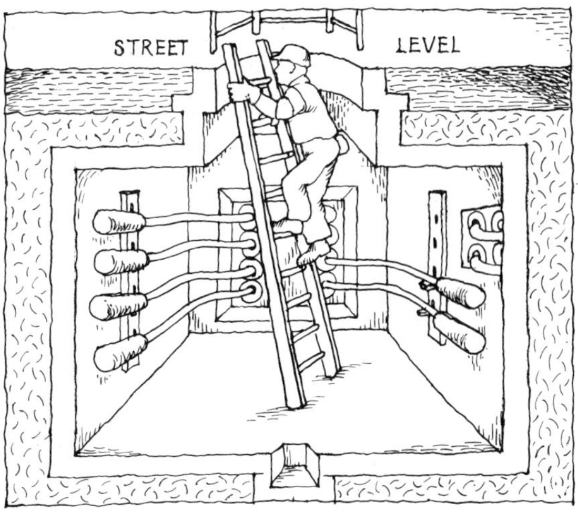

trucks or equipment present and try to determine which of the city's utility systems he is tending.

Where Did All Those Pigeons Come From?

It is fairly common knowledge that when the early settlers came to America they brought along domestic animals such as ducks, chickens, pigs, and cows to provide them with a food supply. Less well known is the fact that they brought along pigeons, also known as rock doves.

The oldest known record showing that pigeons were used for food appears in a carving on a 5,000-year-old Egyptian tomb. In ancient Greece, carrier pigeons were used to spread the news of the Olympic Games to far-flung areas. Back in the twelfth century, the sultan of Baghdad developed a postal system that depended upon pigeons to carry messages. During the Middle Ages, the crusaders employed pigeons to shuttle messages from one castle to another.

By the time our country was settled, pigeons were being raised in European, Asian, and African countries, where they nested under the eaves of country cottages or in the rafters of barns. Sometimes their owners built them elegant houses called dovecotes. Pigeons were easy to keep because they took care of their own needs, feeding on weeds, seeds, and grains that they collected for themselves.

Their life-style continued much the same in America, where farmers often constructed special openings in barns to make it easy for them to come and go. They thrived on grain that spilled in the barnyard as well as on the leftovers remaining in the fields after the harvest. Some were trained for carrying messages, while others were kept as pets. Still others were trained for sport—as racing pigeons. The farmers also liked them because the young birds, called squabs, made delicious eating.

During the 1800s, at about the same time that the government was publishing articles on how to get rid of house sparrows and starlings, articles were also appearing telling people how to raise pigeons and squabs for money. Soon, however, a problem developed. The pigeons began straying from farm to farm. When a cow or turkey wandered off to a neighboring farm, the farmer would fetch it home. But pigeons were much more difficult to capture, and the farmers soon stopped trying.

The pigeons continued to move from farm to farm, and eventually some of them moved into the cities. Here they fed on grain and other food that dropped on the sidewalk, and on food that people put out for them. They had been living with people for so long that they were very tame and brave about accepting handouts. City folks, who missed the animals they had known when they lived in the country, were amused by the bluish gray birds with their iridescent feathers and their bright pink feet. They fed them on windowsills and in parks. The pigeons found church towers and turrets to nest in.

Some big city newspapers even built pigeon lofts atop their buildings. A reporter would take a pigeon along with him on assignment. He would write his story on a thin piece of paper, roll it up, and slip it into a tube attached to a leather harness nestled beneath the pigeon's feathers. The bird would hightail it on back to the loft on the newspaper building, arriving within minutes, unhampered by traffic jams and other urban delays. Nowadays, walkie-talkies and two-way radios serve much the same purpose.

Today, pigeons continue to populate the cities, but they are no longer considered amusing. Many cities have as many pigeons as people. There are so many pigeons that their droppings create a health hazard, because they carry bacteria and viruses that cause disease in humans.

Pigeons multiply rapidly. The male and female choose one mate for life. The female lays her eggs in pairs (the second egg follows the first by about two days), and in seventeen days they hatch. The male and female take turns sitting on the eggs. When the squabs are three weeks old, they weigh more than either of their parents and more than they will ever weigh again in their lives. At four weeks, they start to fly, and within days, they are on their own.

In the meantime, the parent birds have started sitting on another pair of eggs. Pigeons often raise five families a year, which is the major reason for the pigeon population explosion. Add to that the fact that young pigeons are ready to start their own families when they are just one year old. Pigeons have an average life span of fifteen years, and some live to be over thirty. That's why today many city dwellers regard pigeons as problems, not pets.

NINE

Out in the Country

A visit to the country can turn your ideas about size and distance upside down. Your home vegetable garden may seem very large to you when you have to weed it, but it certainly shrinks when you compare it to the acres and acres of vegetables you see growing in farmland. Ideas about near and far tend to change, too, when you visit the country. Your neighborhood store might be just around the corner, but in a rural area, it might well be a few miles on down the road. How do you think your life might be different if you lived on a farm instead of in a suburb or city? How do you think the mountains got so high or the caverns so deep? These are some of the questions you might want to ponder when you explore the countryside.

How Big Is an Acre?

An acre is a term used for a piece of land that equals 43,560 square feet. Think of a distance of about one mile. Perhaps it is a mile from your house to your school, to your friend's house, or to the library. (If you have trouble doing this, ask your mother or father to make a suggestion or to clock a distance of one mile in the car with you.) Take a one-mile-long walk and time yourself. Did it take about twenty minutes?

Now imagine a square that is one mile long on each side. If you were to walk from one corner of that square and continue all the way around until you got back to your starting corner, how many miles would you have walked? Take that number and multiply it by the number of minutes it took you to walk a mile. Now you know how long it would take you to walk around the square.

Think about this: 640 acres fit into a square mile. If it takes you eighty minutes to walk around a one-mile square, it also takes you eighty minutes to walk around an area of 640 acres. If you were a farmer with 640 acres of fields to fence in, you would need four miles of fencing!

Another way to try to visualize the size of an acre is to think of a football field. A football field measures 360 feet by 160 feet. That's 57,600 square feet. In other words, a football field is equal to about one-and-one-third acres of land.

In 1986, crops were harvested from 312,578,000 acres of American land. That's a lot of football fields!

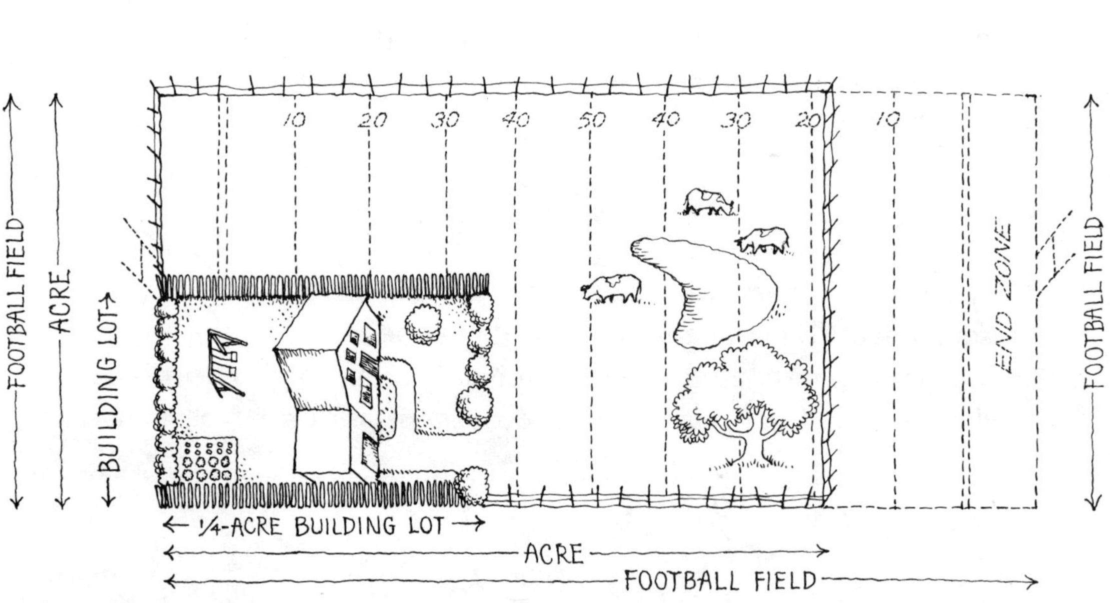

On the Farm

Today, less than 2 percent of the American population works on farms and ranches, yet these people raise enough food to feed everyone in the country, as well as a surplus to ship abroad. In 1985, the U.S.A. produced 13 percent of the world's wheat, 46.9 percent of its corn, and nearly 60 percent of its soybeans. In the 1920s, when your grandparents or great-grandparents were growing up, about one-third of the population worked in agriculture. The major reason that it is now possible for so few people to feed so many is that much of the farm work that used to be done by hand is now done by machinery. Back then, each potato and beet, for example, had to be dug up individually. Now farmers rely on sophisticated harvesting machines designed especially to gather underground crops.

When you travel through farmland, keep a list of the equipment you see. The most obvious machine, present on just about every farm, is the tractor. Some tractors are small, hardly bigger than a ride-on lawnmower, while others are huge machines complete with an air-conditioned enclosed cabin. Depending upon the time of the year and the task at hand, additional machines are often attached to the tractor.

In the spring, the land must be prepared for planting. The tractor pulls a plow, which cuts the soil into chunks and turns it over. Then the plow is replaced by a harrow, whose small circular blades or sharp teeth loosen and pulverize the soil before smoothing and leveling it. After harrowing, the fields are planted. Seed is loaded into a grain drill or planter, which is pulled behind the tractor. The seeds fall to the ground in neat rows. The same machine can also be used to apply fertilizer, either during planting or by itself later.

As the plants begin to grow, the farmer may attach a cultivator to the tractor. This piece of equipment is designed to move between the rows of plants, digging up weeds that could choke the crop and at the same time aerating the soil and helping to keep moisture in. A machine with long arms called a field sprayer is sometimes attached to the tractor during growing season, to spread pesticides on the crops. Airplanes are also used for distributing pesticides.

When the crop is ready to harvest, a wonderful machine called a combine is attached to the tractor. This piece gets its name from the fact that it can "combine" all the steps involved in harvesting grains such as barley and wheat. It pulls the stalks from the ground and removes the grain from them in a process called

CHISEL PLOW

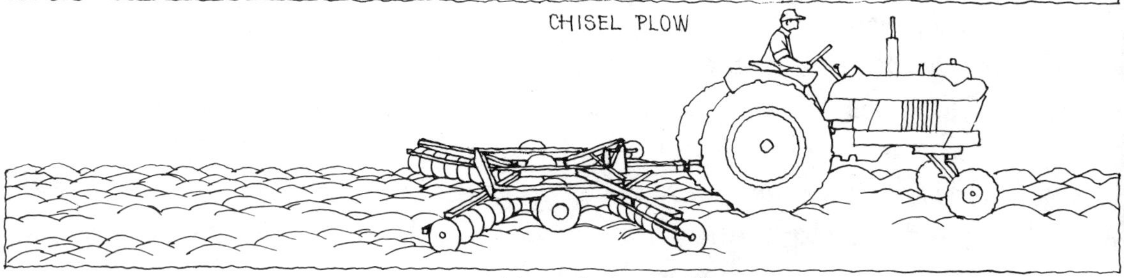

DISC HARROW

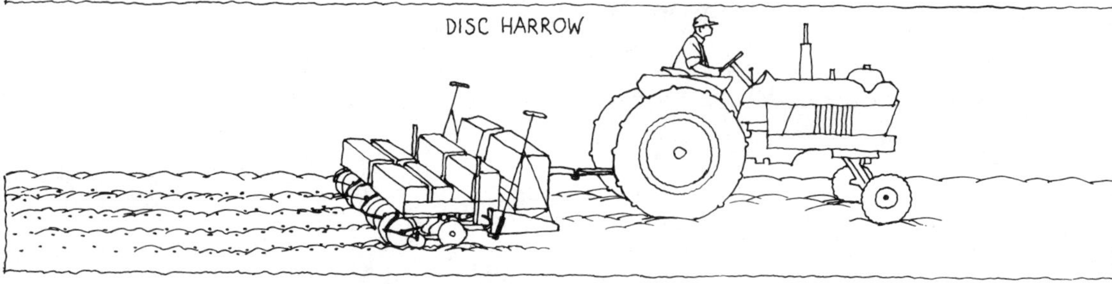

SEED DRILL

threshing. The broken stalks or straw fall back onto the ground while the grain remains in the combine, where it is ground before being transferred to a truck through a pipe. The ground-up grain is taken to a silo, where it is stored until it is either further ground into flour or used as animal feed.

Harvest is certainly the busiest time of year for the farmer. The grain has to be gathered before the onset of winter. Modern technology makes it possible for the farmer to work around the clock when the weather threatens to ruin crops. Sophisticated tractors and other machinery, like the giant irrigation sprayers that pump water onto the land when there is not enough rain, are often equipped with powerful lights for nighttime work.

In your travels, you may see hay being harvested. The tractor

FOUR-ROW CULTIVATOR

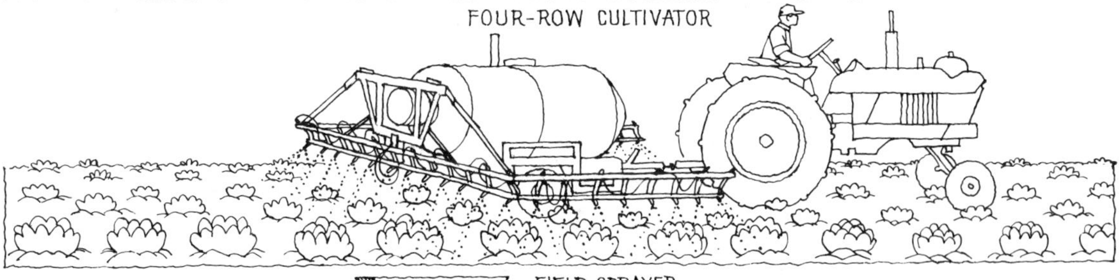

FIELD SPRAYER

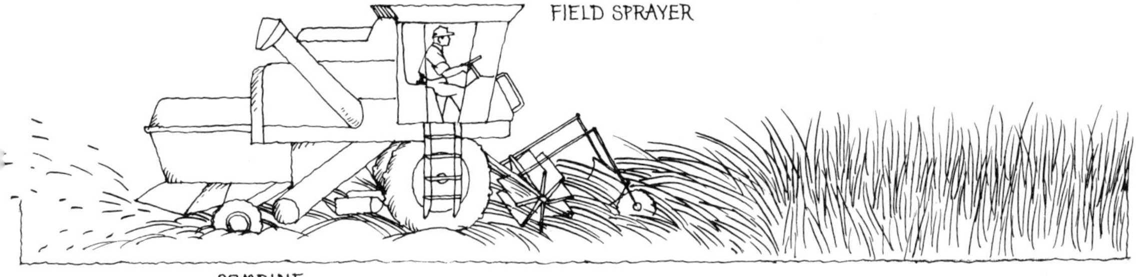

COMBINE

will pull a larger mowing machine with sharp blades that cut the grass close to the ground, where it is left to dry in the sun. Then a hay rake is attached to the tractor and pulled over the rows of cut grass to fluff it up and turn it over so it can dry evenly. The dried grass is called hay, and it is used to feed livestock, especially during the winter when they cannot graze.

Once the hay is cut, the farmer attaches a baler to the tractor. Sometimes a large wagon is also attached behind the baler, so that the whole combination of machines begins to resemble a small train. The baler moves up and down the windrows (rows of hay), picking up the hay, packing it together, and tying it into blocks or bales that can be stored conveniently. It then flips the completed bales into the wagon—no easy task, since a four-foot-by-five-foot bale weighs 850 pounds.

In some parts of the country, farmers use machines that produce round bales. They might also use a stack wagon, which makes tightly compressed stacks of hay with rounded tops. In both cases, the outer layer protects the hay inside, which stays green and fresh and healthful for animals no matter what the weather. The stacks are often used when there is not enough space to store the crop indoors. The stacks shed rain and snow and keep the hay inside fresh for a full year.

The Modern Dairy Farm

Modern technology has made big changes in the way dairy farms operate. When your grandparents were young, each cow was milked by hand. Today, milking is done almost entirely by machine.

The cow enters a special room called a milking parlor, where a farmhand washes her teats before attaching the milking machine.

There are many types of machines, but most work on the same principle. Four rubber tubes dangle from an electric suction pump, which is connected to a small tank or, in the case of a very large farm, to an overhead pipe leading to a bulk tank. Caps on the end of each tube are slipped onto each of the cow's teats. When the power is turned on, the pump sucks the milk out through the tubing. Cows are milked twice a day, and the machines and pipes are sterilized after each milking.

On the modern dairy farm, each cow lives in a stall fitted with a steel stanchion. The cow's head fits through the stanchion, preventing her from wandering off, but she has enough room to move about a bit and to lie down. She always has access to fresh water and she receives a nutritious diet, a combination of ingredients often including steamed yellow corn, wheat bran, dried grains, corn gluten, linseed meal, soybean meal, crimped oats, dehydrated alfalfa meal, ground oats, hominy, molasses, salt, calcium carbonate, vitamin A, and irradiated yeast. The amount of feed a cow receives is determined by the amount of milk she produces. A healthy cow gives about forty pounds of milk a day. Prize milkers sometimes provide up to twice that much. Smaller breeds, such as Jersey cows, give less milk, but it is richer.

The Produce Picture

Different parts of the country have different climates and soil conditions, which means that they are suited to different kinds of crops. Enormous refrigerator trailer trucks make it possible to safely transport delicate produce to supermarkets hundreds and even thousands of miles away safely and quickly. Huge cargo planes ship out-of-season produce from farms in the South and West to the supermarkets in the Midwest and East in a matter of hours. The next time you go to the supermarket, ask the produce manager where some of the fruits and vegetables come from. If you live in New England, for example, you may be surprised to learn that your salad last night included tomatoes from Georgia and lettuce from California.

Shipping food adds to its price. Try making a chart to keep track of the prices of fruits or vegetables you like. Track them month by month. You may find that strawberries, peaches, or corn on the cob are not available during certain months of the year. You may also find that, if they are available, they don't taste as good at certain times of year as at others. That might be because they've been in storage for a long time and are not so fresh.

When you travel to different states or different parts of the country, it's fun to pay a visit to the produce section of a local supermarket. Compare the prices of your list items in those markets and in your supermarket at home. Then try to answer these questions:

- Are there some foods in the produce section of the new supermarket that you don't find at home?
- Are the foods native to a region cheaper or more expensive than those that have to be shipped in?
- How does the cost of a locally grown product change as the season changes?
- Do foods sold at roadside stands tend to be more or less expensive than those found in the supermarket? How does the quality compare?
- When you go to a restaurant, are there items on the menu that you don't usually see at home? Is that because they contain foods that are readily available in this part of the country but not where you live?

If you would like to pick your own strawberries straight from the field or pluck your own apples in an orchard, write ahead to the tourist information bureau or the department of agriculture in the state you plan to visit, requesting a list of pick-your-own farms. (See the chapter called Planning Your Trip, pages 1–9, for advice on getting the addresses you need.)

Mountains

Mountains are formed by heat and pressure from very hot rock inside the earth. Over a period of millions of years, the heat within cracks the earth's crust and forces up the great bands and peaks of rock that we call mountains. Climate can vary drastically in a mountainous area. The warm air from the surrounding land rises into the atmosphere and meets cold air. That's why it's possible to have, on the same mountain, a tropical rain forest on the low-lying slopes and an ice-covered peak where it is too cold for any trees to survive.

There are three kinds of mountains in the world, all of them resulting from activity in the earth's crust. The largest mountains, including the Rockies in the western United States, are the fastest-forming kind. They are made by volcanoes within the earth, which force hot rock to pour out and form tall cones. Such mountains are made from igneous rock, the only kind of rock there was when the earth was formed. Originating deep within the earth, igneous rock is harder than other rock, and can be found in the red-hot lava produced by volcanos still active today. Granite is an igneous rock, and because it is so hard it lasts a long time. That's why it is favored as a building material.

Block mountains develop along cracks or "faults" in the earth's crust. The land on one side of the crack slips downward, making the other side rise above like a great stone cliff. When there are two cracks fairly close to each other, the land between the two is sometimes forced up to form a long row of block mountains. If the two cracks are hundreds of miles apart, the raised area in between is called a plateau. If the land in between sinks down, it is called a rift valley.

The third kind are called fold mountains. They are like huge zigzag wrinkles, formed as the earth's crust is squeezed from the sides. Layers of soil and rock on the surface fold over as they are pressed together, piling up higher and higher over a period of millions of years. Sedimentary rocks are common here. This is rock formed from thousands of tiny bits of sand, shells, and clay. It collects in layers, called sediment, on the floor of oceans and lakes. As millions of years pass, the layers of sediment, pressured by the immense weight of the waters above, fuse together into layers of solid rock.

When an animal or plant gets buried in the sediment and rots

THE SIERRA NEVADA MOUNTAINS ARE BLOCK MOUNTAINS.

away, an impression of its shape is left behind, just as your foot leaves a print in wet sand at the beach. Such shapes, found in the layers of rock, are called fossils. By comparing them, geologists can determine the age of the rocks. Mountain climbers have located fossils of sea creatures thousands of feet above the earth's surface, which provides evidence that many mountains were made beneath the sea.

The earth is 45 million years old, and it is very possible that some mountains may still be growing. And yet, they may not be getting any bigger. That's because the forces of erosion—the ice, wind, and rain that wear them away—tend to counteract any growth. If you visit a national park, you'll find rules against picking or trampling on fragile plants. One reason for that is the need to preserve unusual types of vegetation. Another reason is that the plans can help to slow erosion by keeping the rain from washing away loose rock and soil.

Last Thoughts

You don't need to go far to enjoy the rewards of travel. There are sights, sounds, smells, and tastes to discover all around. If you are a traveler at heart, what is important is not how many miles you stray but how much you experience. Being a true traveler is a matter of attitude. It's a matter of searching out new places to visit, and it's also a matter of revisiting the familiar ones with a fresh eye.

Many of the projects in *Going Places* can be undertaken at home. Some will help you prepare for a trip while others will enable you to learn more about familiar locations. Pretty soon you'll find that you're making new discoveries on short trips as well as on long ones.

Wherever you go, add to your store of impressions by talking to the people you meet. Ask the waitress in the diner to point out the most popular dessert on the menu and then give it a try. Drop in at a local library and ask the librarian to tell you a little about the statue in the nearby park. Zookeepers and museum guides are also great sources of information, as are forest rangers and airline attendants.

With *Going Places,* you'll be able to become an active participant in every trip you take, from start to finish. Have a terrific journey, whether it be to a neighboring city or the other side of the country. Bon voyage!

Index